IMMIGRATION IN THE 21ST CENTURY:
POLITICAL, SOCIAL AND ECONOMIC ISSUES

MIGRATION OF UNACCOMPANIED CHILDREN FROM CENTRAL AMERICA

CAUSES, ASSISTANCE AND EFFECTIVENESS

IMMIGRATION IN THE 21ST CENTURY: POLITICAL, SOCIAL AND ECONOMIC ISSUES

Additional books in this series can be found on Nova's website
under the Series tab.

Additional e-books in this series can be found on Nova's website
under the e-book tab.

IMMIGRATION IN THE 21ST CENTURY:
POLITICAL, SOCIAL AND ECONOMIC ISSUES

MIGRATION OF UNACCOMPANIED CHILDREN FROM CENTRAL AMERICA

CAUSES, ASSISTANCE AND EFFECTIVENESS

ANGIE HOPKINS
EDITOR

nova publishers
New York

Library of Congress Cataloging-in-Publication Data

ISBN: 978-1-63484-604-2

Published by Nova Science Publishers, Inc. † New York

Contents

PREFACE

U.S. agencies have sought to address causes of unaccompanied alien child (UAC) migration through recent programs, such as information campaigns to deter migration, developed in response to the migration increase and other long-standing efforts. The recent migration increase was likely triggered, according to U.S. officials, by several emergent factors such as the increased presence and sophistication of human smugglers (known as coyotes) and confusion over U.S. immigration policy. Officials also noted that certain persistent conditions such as violence and poverty have worsened in certain countries. In addition to long-standing efforts, such as U.S. Agency for International Development (USAID) antipoverty programs, agencies have taken new actions. For example, Department of Homeland Security (DHS)-led investigative units have increasingly sought to disrupt human smuggling operations. This book reviews U.S. assistance in El Salvador, Guatemala, and Honduras addressing agency-identified causes of UAC migration; how agencies have determined where to locate these assistance efforts; and the extent to which agencies have developed processes to assess the effectiveness of programs seeking to address UAC migration.

In: Migration of Unaccompanied Children … ISBN: 978-1-63484-604-2
Editor: Angie Hopkins

Chapter 1

CENTRAL AMERICA: IMPROVED EVALUATION EFFORTS COULD ENHANCE AGENCY PROGRAMS TO REDUCE UNACCOMPANIED CHILD MIGRATION*

United States Government Accountability Office

WHY GAO DID THIS STUDY

According to DHS, the number of UAC apprehended at the U.S.-Mexican border climbed from nearly 28,000 in fiscal year 2012 to more than 73,000 in fiscal year 2014, with nearly three- fourths of those apprehended nationals of El Salvador, Guatemala, and Honduras. Children from these three countries face a host of challenges, such as extreme violence and persistent poverty. Those who migrate can encounter even more dangers, such as robbery and abuse.

GAO was asked to review issues related to UAC migration. In February 2015, GAO reported on U.S. assistance to Central America addressing the rapid increase in UAC migration. This report reviews (1) U.S. assistance in El Salvador, Guatemala, and Honduras addressing agency- identified causes of

---

* This is an edited, reformatted and augmented version of the United States Government Accountability Office publication, GAO-15-707, dated July 2015.

UAC migration; (2) how agencies have determined where to locate these assistance efforts; and (3) the extent to which agencies have developed processes to assess the effectiveness of programs seeking to address UAC migration. GAO reviewed agency documents and interviewed officials in Washington, D.C., and in Central America.

WHAT GAO RECOMMENDS

GAO recommends that DHS and State take steps to integrate evaluations into their planning for, and implementation of, future information campaigns intended to deter migration. GAO also recommends that DHS establish performance targets for its investigative units. DHS concurred with both recommendations, and State concurred with the one recommendation directed to it.

WHAT GAO FOUND

U.S. agencies have sought to address causes of unaccompanied alien child (UAC) migration through recent programs, such as information campaigns to deter migration, developed in response to the migration increase and other long- standing efforts. The recent migration increase was likely triggered, according to U.S. officials, by several emergent factors such as the increased presence and sophistication of human smugglers (known as coyotes) and confusion over U.S. immigration policy. Officials also noted that certain persistent conditions such as violence and poverty have worsened in certain countries. In addition to long- standing efforts, such as U.S. Agency for International Development (USAID) antipoverty programs, agencies have taken new actions. For example, Department of Homeland Security (DHS)-led investigative units have increasingly sought to disrupt human smuggling operations.

U.S. agencies have located programs based on various factors, including long- term priorities such as targeting high-poverty and -crime areas, but have adjusted to locate more programs in high-migration communities. For example, Department of State (State) officials in Guatemala said they moved programs enhancing police anticrime capabilities into such communities, and

USAID officials in El Salvador said they expanded to UAC-migration-affected locations.

Most agencies have developed processes to assess the effectiveness of programs seeking to address UAC migration, but weaknesses exist in these processes for some antismuggling programs. For example, DHS has established performance measures, such as arrests, for units combating UAC smuggling, but has not established numeric or other types of targets for these measures, which would enable DHS to measure the units' progress. In addition, DHS and State have not always evaluated information campaigns intended to combat coyote misinformation. DHS launched its 2013 campaign in April, but launched its 2014 campaign in late June after migration levels peaked. Neither agency evaluated its 2014 campaign. Collecting performance information on media campaigns can have value in informing future campaign efforts to reduce child migration.

ABBREVIATIONS

CARSI	Central America Regional Security Initiative
CBP	U.S. Customs and Border Protection
CDCS	Country Development Cooperation Strategy
DHS	Department of Homeland Security
DOJ	Department of Justice
IAF	Inter-American Foundation
ICE	U.S. Immigration and Customs Enforcement
INL	Bureau of International Narcotics and Law Enforcement Affairs
MCC	Millennium Challenge Corporation
NGO	nongovernmental organization
PMP	Performance Management Plan
PPR	Performance Plan and Report
State	Department of State
TCIU	Transnational Criminal Investigative Unit
UAC	unaccompanied alien child(ren)
USAID	U.S. Agency for International Development
WHA	Western Hemisphere Affairs

July 29, 2015

Congressional Requesters

Since 2012, there has been a rapid increase in the number of apprehensions at the U.S.-Mexican border of unaccompanied alien children (UAC)—foreign nationals under the age of 18 who are neither with a parent nor with a legal guardian at the time they are apprehended.[1] According to the Department of Homeland Security (DHS), the number of UAC from any country apprehended at the U.S. border climbed from nearly 28,000 in fiscal year 2012 to more than 42,000 in fiscal year 2013, and to more than 73,000 in fiscal year 2014. Prior to fiscal year 2012, most UAC apprehended at the border were Mexican nationals. However, starting in fiscal year 2013, the total number of UAC from El Salvador, Guatemala, and Honduras surpassed the number of UAC from Mexico and, in fiscal year 2014, far surpassed the number of UAC from Mexico.

Children from El Salvador, Guatemala, and Honduras face a host of perils both within their countries and along the migration route to the United States. In February, we reported that U.S. officials in El Salvador, Guatemala, and Honduras most commonly identified crime and violence and economic concerns as among the primary causes of UAC migration to the United States.[2] These three countries have among the world's highest murder rates, according to the United Nations Office on Drugs and Crime, along with a widespread presence of gangs in each, as well as high poverty rates and a number of other persistent problems that diminish living conditions. Children who migrate, however, can encounter further risks, with some having to travel over a thousand miles to the U.S. border, sometimes crossing the desert by foot or riding on top of trains. Along the way, they can encounter numerous dangers, including robbery, extortion, abandonment, rape, or murder.

A number of U.S. agencies provide assistance intended to improve living conditions and strengthen rule of law in the three countries, including the U.S. Agency for International Development (USAID); the Departments of State (State), Homeland Security (DHS) and Justice (DOJ), the Millennium Challenge Corporation (MCC);[3] and the Inter-American Foundation (IAF).[4] The U.S. government also provides additional assistance through the Central America Regional Security Initiative (CARSI). In its fiscal year 2016 budget request, the administration requested an additional $1 billion for Central America to support assistance efforts intended to address underlying causes of migration.

We were asked to review a number of issues related to UAC migration. We recently reported on U.S. efforts to screen and care for UAC migrants who safely arrive at the border,[5] and we plan to report in 2016 on efforts to care for UAC once in U.S. custody. This report reviews (1) U.S. assistance in El Salvador, Guatemala, and Honduras addressing agency- identified causes of UAC migration; (2) how agencies have determined where to locate these assistance efforts; and (3) the extent to which agencies have developed processes to assess the effectiveness of programs seeking to address UAC migration.

To address the objectives for this review, we obtained written responses from agency officials outlining what they identified as the causes of UAC migration, and actions taken in response to the migration increase. To assess these responses, we reviewed agency documents for programs agencies identified as addressing causes of UAC migration, including country and program strategies, operational plans, project proposal and appraisal documents, and progress reports, among others. We also interviewed U.S. and nongovernment officials in Washington, D.C., and U.S., host government, and nongovernment officials in El Salvador, Guatemala, and Honduras, where we also visited U.S. agency-supported projects and met with children in each country. For more information on our scope and methodology, see appendix I.

We conducted this performance audit from September 2014 to July 2015 in accordance with generally accepted government auditing standards. Those standards require that we plan and perform the audit to obtain sufficient, appropriate evidence to provide a reasonable basis for our findings and conclusions based on our audit objectives. We believe that the evidence obtained provides a reasonable basis for our findings and conclusions based on our audit objectives.

BACKGROUND

Since 2012, there has been a rapid increase in the number of UAC apprehended at the U.S.-Mexican border. According to DHS's U.S. Customs and Border Protection (CBP), the number of UAC from any country apprehended at the border climbed from nearly 28,000 in fiscal year 2012 to more than 42,000 in fiscal year 2013, and to more than 73,000 in fiscal year 2014. Prior to fiscal year 2012, the majority of UAC apprehended at the border were Mexican nationals.[6] However, as figure 1 shows, more than half of the UAC apprehended at the border in fiscal year 2013, and nearly three-fourths of

UAC apprehended in fiscal year 2014, were nationals of El Salvador, Guatemala, and Honduras.[7]

Recent data indicate the pace of migration from Central America remains high, though fewer migrants are being apprehended in the United States. According to DHS's Border Patrol—a component of CBP—through May 2015, there have been nearly 23,000 UAC apprehensions at the southwest border in fiscal year 2015—compared with about 24,500 through May of fiscal year 2013 and nearly 47,000 through May of fiscal year 2014. However, according to research from the nongovernmental organization (NGO) the Washington Office on Latin America, Central American migrants are being detained in Mexico at a higher rate this year compared with last year, with more than 90,000 Central American migrants detained in Mexico during the first 7 months of fiscal year 2015 compared with around 50,000 during the same period of fiscal year 2014. Since 2012, apprehensions of UAC at the U.S.-Mexican border have generally increased between January and May, as shown in figure 2, according to data from DHS's Border Patrol.

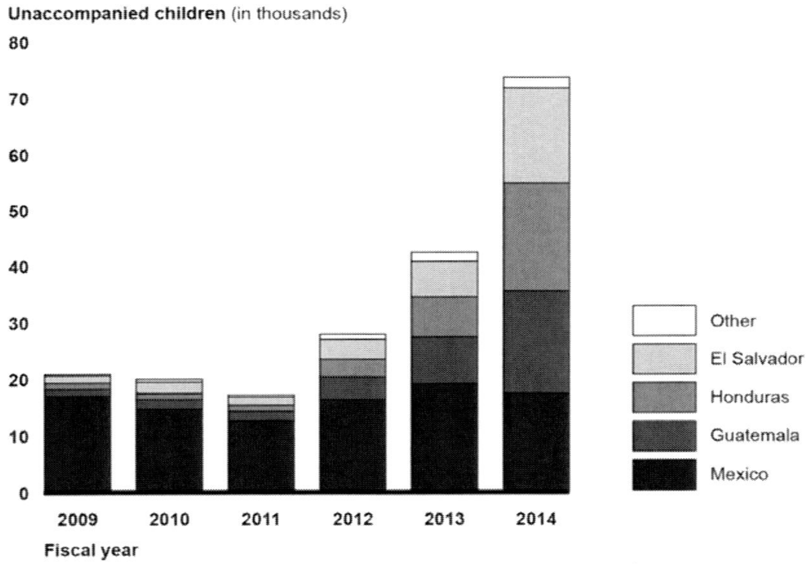

Source: GAO analysis of Department of Homeland Security data. | GAO-15-507

Figure 1. Apprehensions of Unaccompanied Alien Children by Country of Citizenship, Fiscal Years 2009 through 2014.

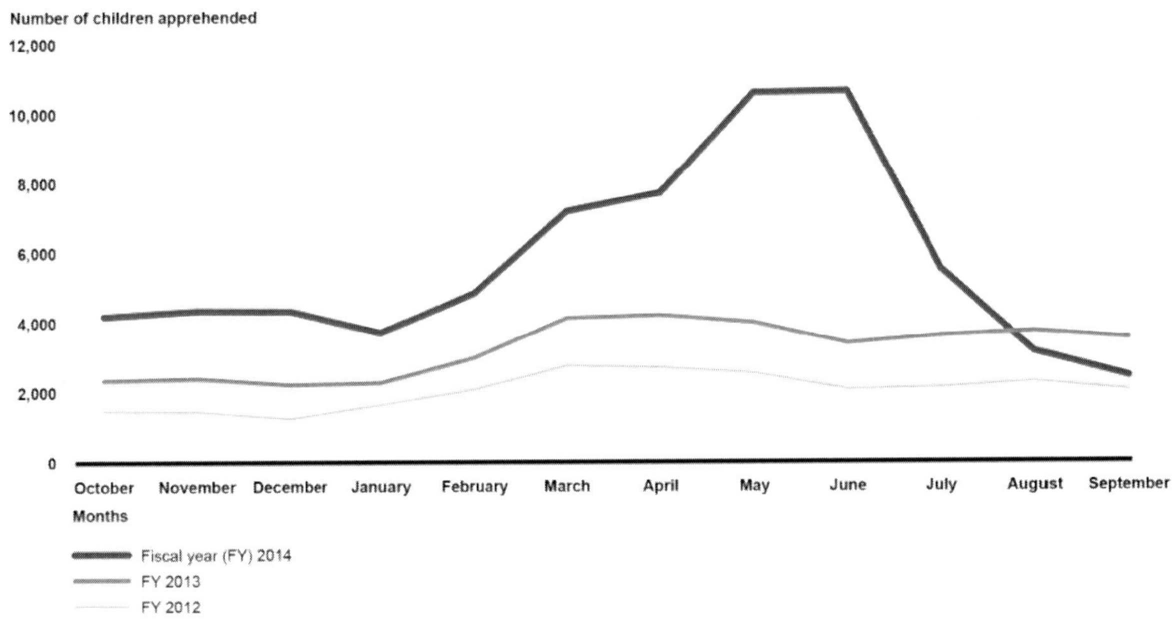

Source: GAO analysis of Department of Homeland Security data. | GAO-15-507

Figure 2. Apprehensions of Unaccompanied Alien Children at the U.S-Mexican Border, by Month, Fiscal Years 2012-2014.

These three countries face a variety of socioeconomic challenges. In February 2015, we reported that U.S. officials in El Salvador, Guatemala, and Honduras identified crime and violence, and economic and educational concerns, as among the primary causes of UAC migration to the United States.[8] According to the United Nations Office on Drugs and Crime, these countries had among the top five highest homicide rates worldwide in 2012, the most recent year for which these statistics were available for all three countries, with Honduras ranking first, with a homicide rate of 90.4 per 100,000 inhabitants; El Salvador fourth, with a rate of 41.2; and Guatemala fifth, with a rate of 39.9. According to this UN office, the surge in homicide levels in Central America in recent years is largely a result of violence related to the control of drug trafficking routes, turf wars between criminal groups, and conflict between organized criminal groups and the host government.[9] A 2014 United Nations High Commissioner for Refugees study on UAC from Central America and Mexico noted that nearly half of the UAC interviewed for the study reported being affected by violence committed by gangs or drug cartels, while about a fifth reported being victims of domestic abuse.[10] In addition, according to 2011 World Bank data, more than 60 percent of Hondurans, more than 50 percent of Guatemalans, and 30 percent of Salvadorans live below the poverty level. According to a Wilson Center publication, nearly 2 million Central Americans between the ages of 15 and 25 do not have a job or go to school,[11] and the highest proportion of these youth come from El Salvador, Guatemala, and Honduras.[12]In addition, all three countries rank below the regional average on Transparency International's Corruption Perception Index.[13]

In September 2014, the governments of El Salvador, Guatemala, and Honduras issued a regional plan in response to the recent migration increase.[14] The plan, referred to as the *Plan of the Alliance for Prosperity in the Northern Triangle: A Road Map*, outlines four strategic actions, which seek to stimulate the productive sector to create economic opportunities, develop opportunities for people, improve public safety and enhance access to the legal system, and strengthen institutions to increase people's trust in the state. The plan notes that income inequality presents a major challenge to the three countries, as 20 percent of the wealthiest segments of the population account for more than half of overall income. In addition, the plan identifies a limited supply and quality of services in housing, early childhood health care, nutrition, and child development as among the main challenges to development, while also noting that weaknesses in the countries' educational systems have resulted in workforces with less schooling and more limited skills as compared with those of other countries in the region.

In addition to the problems within these countries, children who migrate illegally can encounter other risks during the journey to the United States. The journey to the United States may be hundreds or over a thousand miles, and some make this journey on foot over desert terrain, where daytime summer temperatures can exceed 110 degrees Fahrenheit. Others travel on top of trains, such as La Bestia, or "the Beast," the name given to the cargo trains that transport goods through Mexico to the United States. According to NGO reports, whether traveling by foot or on trains, child migrants are exposed to various dangers, including robbery, extortion, forced recruitment into gangs, abandonment, rape, and murder.

A number of U.S. agencies provide assistance to the three countries. For example, USAID, State,[15] DHS,[16] IAF, and MCC have programs providing assistance in areas such as economic development, rule of law, citizen security, law enforcement, education, community development, and others. In fiscal year 2014, USAID, State, DHS, and IAF allocated a combined $44.5 million for El Salvador, $88.1 million for Guatemala, and $78 million for Honduras. In addition, MCC signed a threshold program agreement with Honduras in fiscal year 2013 totaling $15.6 million, a compact agreement with El Salvador in fiscal year 2014 totaling $277 million, and a threshold program agreement with Guatemala in fiscal year 2015 totaling $28 million.[17] The U.S. government also provides additional assistance through CARSI, which funds activities to improve law enforcement and justice sector capabilities, prevent crime and violence, and deter and detect border criminal activity, among other efforts in these three countries as well as in Belize, Costa Rica, Nicaragua, and Panama. Between fiscal years 2008 and 2014, U.S. agencies allocated more than $800 million for CARSI activities from various accounts. We previously reported that, through June 2013, more than 50 percent of funds allocated for CARSI activities had been designated for activities in El Salvador, Guatemala, and Honduras.[18] Additional information on agency funding to the three countries is provided in appendix II.

The administration has taken several recent actions related to these three countries. In December 2014, the administration started an in-country refugee and parole program, which is intended to allow certain parents who are lawfully present in the United States to request access to the U.S. Refugee Admissions Program for their children still living in El Salvador, Guatemala, and Honduras. In addition, in March 2015, the administration issued the U.S. Strategy for Engagement in Central America, which includes the primary objectives of prosperity, governance, and security, and goals of an economically integrated Central America that is fully democratic; provides economic opportunities to its people; enjoys more accountable, transparent, and effective public institutions; and ensures a safe environment for its citizens.[19] According to the strategy, important successes would include the establishment of strong regional coordination mechanisms and institutions; reducing violence to a point where no Central American country is among the top 10 countries in terms of homicide rates; a 50 percent reduction of the youth unemployment rate in Honduras, El Salvador, and Guatemala; full implementation of ongoing electrical interconnection projects and other initiatives aimed at making energy more affordable, cleaner, and more sustainable; and steady economic growth throughout the region such that the poverty rate is pushed to below 40 percent over the next decade.

In its fiscal year 2016 budget request, the administration requested $1 billion for Central America, an increase of more than 200 percent from fiscal year 2014 levels. State and USAID have stated that the funding would support the U.S. Strategy for Engagement in Central America and the priority objectives identified in the Alliance for Prosperity Plan. According to agency budget documents, funding would seek to address the underlying factors of undocumented migration from Central America, among other priorities.

Agencies Seek to Address Causes of UAC Migration with Recently Developed and Long-standing Efforts

Agency officials noted that the rapid increase in UAC migration is due to several emergent factors, including the proliferation of human smugglers, or coyotes. Agencies have taken some actions in response to the rapid increase in migration, including several intended to directly reduce illegal migration and combat coyotes. In addition, agencies have a number of long-standing efforts, developed prior to the increase in migration, that seek to address pervasive violence, poverty, and other conditions agencies also identified as contributing to migration.

A Mixture of Emergent Factors and Pervasive Problems Likely Triggered the Rapid Increase in Migration, According to Officials

Agency officials noted that a variety of factors likely caused the recent rapid increase in UAC migration, including the increased presence of coyotes, perceptions concerning U.S. immigration law, and recent improvements in the U.S. economy. In addition, agency officials noted that some pervasive problems have recently intensified in some places, including rising levels of violence and insecurity and worsening economic and social conditions.

Emergent Factors

All agency officials we spoke with from all three countries identified several emergent factors as likely triggering the rapid increase in migration, including the growing presence of coyotes as one of the top factors. Agency officials from all three countries that we spoke to said that coyotes had proliferated and grown more influential and sophisticated in recent years. Officials from USAID and State in all three countries noted that coyotes were often well known and trusted in communities. According to USAID officials, when they conducted focus group interviews in Honduras with youth and outreach center coordinators in high-risk communities, including San Pedro Sula,[20] participants noted that coyotes were easy to access. In addition, agency officials we spoke to in all three countries noted that coyotes had instituted new marketing and messaging tactics. For example, numerous officials in all three countries told us that coyotes offered package deals, such as offering three attempts to migrate to the United States for one fee—known as a "three-for-one" deal. Coyotes have also intentionally spread rumors and misinformation about U.S. immigration policy. For example, agency officials told us that, in some cases, in an effort to drive smuggling business, coyotes led many people to believe children could migrate to the United States and receive permission to stay indefinitely, if they arrived by a certain date.

According to agency officials, general perceptions concerning U.S. immigration policy have played a growing role in UAC migration. Agency officials noted they relied on outreach efforts, focus groups, and other information sources to try to understand this factor. According to State officials in El Salvador and Guatemala, local media outlets have optimistically discussed comprehensive immigration reform efforts in the United States and sometimes failed to discuss the complexity of immigration reform. According to State officials, many Guatemalan citizens believe undocumented migrants in the United States will be encouraged to send for their children from Guatemala so they can come to the United States and they can benefit together for any upcoming comprehensive immigration reform, or even be eligible for Deferred Action for Childhood Arrivals.[21] In addition, according to USAID officials, Honduran youth and coordinators of community centers who were interviewed as part of a USAID focus group indicated they believed the United States would allow migrant minors, mothers traveling with minors, and pregnant women to stay for a period of time upon arrival in the United States.

Agency officials also noted that recent improvements in the U.S. economy had fueled increased UAC migration, enabling family reunification in the United States. In particular, State and USAID officials in Honduras noted that the improving economy had enabled parents who immigrated to the United States to send money back to their home country to pay coyotes so their children could migrate and reunify the family in the United States.

According to officials in El Salvador, as the economy improved there, more Salvadorans have attempted to migrate to the United States to reunify with family. Agency officials noted that many children have spent years apart from their parents, being raised by a grandparent or another family member, and that in some cases, aging grandparents were no longer able to care for the children. This dynamic is further illustrated by examples from an internal USAID analysis of migration causes in Honduras, which highlighted migration-related risk factors associated with children living with extended family or non-family members in Honduras.

Some agency officials also noted that the increased use of social media has enabled migrating families to be in more regular contact and to confirm if and when family members or friends arrive in the United States. Additionally, according to a study performed by State contractors in El Salvador, many people advertise immigration services through social media and offer travel services to ensure safe arrival in the United States. The use of social media can encourage migration, according to some agency officials. For example, officials in Guatemala noted that social media outlets enable migrants who have arrived in the United States to share messages and pictures with families in their home countries, an act that can serve as a powerful and influential endorsement of the decision to migrate. Agency officials in El Salvador similarly noted that when a potential migrant hears from someone in the United States who has managed to arrive and remain there undocumented, the communication can strongly influence their decision on whether to migrate.

Worsening of Pervasive Socio- economic Problems

Violence, poverty, and poor access to education and other services have been pervasive development challenges in all three countries, predating the UAC migration increase. However, according to agency officials we spoke to in all three countries, some of these problems have grown worse in recent years and could have contributed to the rise of UAC migration. For example, in Honduras, agency officials noted that levels and perceptions of violence had grown worse, in part because of the rise in extortions. Worsening security concerns also negatively affect access to education. For example, agency officials in El Salvador noted that many children will not attend school after the seventh grade because traveling to some schools requires crossing gang borders, and that girls in particular face the risk of being attacked or raped en route. In Guatemala, agency officials stated that poor economic and social conditions in the Western Highlands had declined even further in recent years.[22] In addition, agency officials noted that deteriorating climate conditions, including several consecutive years of drought and a coffee rust blight that has hurt coffee production and cost jobs in Honduras and Guatemala, exacerbated long-standing economic concerns in many communities. Agency officials told us that, on the basis of their outreach efforts, reporting from NGOs, academics, and government officials, and focus groups, they had determined that these longstanding problems had intensified.

In addition, we met with children from all three countries who offered similar insights concerning the causes of migration.[23] For example, children at a USAID outreach center in San Pedro Sula, Honduras, noted the lack of educational and job opportunities in their communities as a reason for migrating. Children from a particularly violent neighborhood told us it was even more difficult for them to obtain a job because potential employers would sometimes choose not to hire them because of where they live. Children also described the ways in which violence leads to migration, such as by making it difficult for them to attend school if doing so requires them to travel from one neighborhood to another and cross a gang border. Children at an outreach center in El Salvador also noted that sometimes, even with an education, one cannot find work in El Salvador and that there are more opportunities and chances to succeed in the United States. Children at this same center indicated that the desire to migrate is even stronger for children with parents in the United States. Children from a youth center in Guatemala also noted violence and economic factors as motivations for migration, and many of these children already had family or knew someone who had migrated.

Agency Actions Taken in Response to the Migration Increase Include Several Efforts to Combat Child Smuggling

Among the various agency actions taken in response to UAC migration, several seek to directly combat coyotes, which agency officials identified as a key emergent factor causing migration. Agencies also have established efforts to increase legal migration and improve migrant return centers.

Antismuggling Law Enforcement and Legislative Efforts

In response to the increase in UAC migration, DHS and State have supported several law enforcement and legislative outreach efforts that have marked an increased focus on investigating and dismantling smuggling operations in all three countries. For example:

- According to DHS officials from Homeland Security Investigations, in response to the rapid increase in UAC migration in 2014, DHS shifted the investigative priorities of its Transnational Criminal Investigative Units (TCIU) to target child-smuggling operations in all three countries. The units include host government police, customs officers, and prosecutors, among others, and are intended to facilitate information sharing and rapid bilateral investigations involving trafficking of people, money, drugs, and weapons, and other priorities. The units have focused their efforts on seeking to identify and dismantle criminal organizations involved in smuggling. According to DHS and DOJ officials, TCIUs across the three countries coordinate efforts given the transnational nature of the smuggling rings. A DHS official in Guatemala told us the unit there was able to dismantle two of the seven criminal organizations it was investigating that were actively smuggling children. DHS, with State's Bureau of International Narcotics and Law Enforcement (INL) funding, has indicated it plans to increase the size of these units.[24]
- State/INL in Honduras is working with a DOJ resident legal advisor to assist the Honduran attorney general's office in prosecuting trafficking and alien-smuggling cases. This assistance includes, among other things, providing training to Honduran prosecutors on developing cases against smuggling organizations.
- State/INL support in Guatemala has included assistance to reform police training, with a new emphasis on UAC-related issues in the

community policing techniques, criminal investigations, and human rights curricula.

- State has participated in legislative and political outreach efforts to combat smuggling. For example, in Guatemala, State has advocated modifying certain laws that would better enable Guatemalan law enforcement to investigate and prosecute these cases and, if applicable, carry out appropriate penalties for the crimes.

Public Information Campaigns to Deter Migration

DHS and State carried out several public information campaigns between 2013 and 2015 intended to dissuade citizens of El Salvador, Guatemala, and Honduras from migrating to the United States. Between the aforementioned years, DHS carried out three public information campaigns. The campaigns in 2013 and 2014 focused on warning potential migrants of the dangers of the journey, while the 2015 campaign sought to increase awareness of requirements under the executive action on immigration, including Deferred Action for Childhood Arrivals, how it will be implemented, and who is eligible. This campaign was launched in January 2015 but was stopped February 16, 2015, because of a federal court ruling that granted a preliminary injunction to prevent expansion of Deferred Action for Childhood Arrivals, among other things.[25] The campaigns ran in El Salvador, Guatemala, Honduras, and Mexico, with ads placed on radio and TV stations, and on billboards, bus stops, and in and on buses (see figure 3). According to an official from DHS CBP's Office of Public Affairs, in developing the 2013 dangers of the journey campaign, DHS incorporated feedback from various U.S. agencies and a working group composed of several DHS components; the embassies of El Salvador, Guatemala, and Honduras; and other international and nongovernmental organizations. DHS does not currently have an active campaign. The DHS official also noted DHS would like to develop a new campaign for early 2016 if funding is available.

State public affairs officials we spoke to at the U.S embassies in all three countries told us they used the DHS campaign materials and developed their own materials to launch related public information campaigns in- country while also supporting similar host government campaigns. For example, in Honduras the U.S embassy's public affairs section used social media and webinars to provide information on migration, while in Guatemala the public affairs section at the U.S. embassy there placed ads on newspapers, the radio, and buses. In El Salvador, public affairs officials from the U.S embassy collaborated with the host government to develop its message intended to deter migration. In addition, State officials from the consular affairs sections from the U.S. embassies in Guatemala and El Salvador have also made efforts to counter misinformation. In Guatemala, State consular officials from the U.S embassy incorporated UAC-related messages into their regular community presentations, such as by adding Power Point slides addressing the dangers of the journey and the importance of being aware of coyotes, while State consular officers from the U.S. embassy in El Salvador distributed information in consular waiting areas.

In-Country Refugee/Parole Program Intended to Increase Legal Migration

In an effort to increase legal migration and reduce the number of children attempting to migrate to the United States, State and DHS have collaborated to implement a new in-country refugee/parole processing program. The program was announced in November 2014 and began accepting applications the following month. There is currently no deadline for filing an application through this program. Through this program, qualifying parents in the United States can petition on behalf of their children for refugee[26] status and if the child is ineligible for refugee admission but still at risk of harm, the child may be considered for parole on a case-by-case basis.[27] The child must be unmarried; under the age of 21; a national of El Salvador, Guatemala, or Honduras; and residing in his or her country of nationality. Once a parent submits an application through a designated resettlement agency, DNA tests are conducted to prove the biological relationship and the child is interviewed in country by a DHS official to determine whether the child qualifies for refugee status. As of June 2015, State officials in Washington D.C. reported that the program had received 1,385 applications. Of those applications, 1,139 are from El Salvador, 225 from Honduras, and 21 from Guatemala. State officials also reported no interviews have yet been conducted. A DHS official in Guatemala noted DHS needed to improve their advertising of the program to Guatemalan citizens. A State official in Washington, D.C., noted in particular that more information advertising the program in indigenous languages was needed.

Source: Department of Homeland Security. | GAO-15-507
(Left) DHS Dangers of the Journey Campaign Poster. (Translation: "I thought it would be easy for my son to get papers in the North… That wasn't true. Our children are the future: We (must) protect them.") (Right) Photos of campaign posters placed on the back of a bus and on a billboard in Central America.

Figure 3. Images from Department of Homeland Security's Dangers of the Journey Campaign.

Source: GAO. |GAO-15-507
Basic supplies provided to returned migrants (left) and preparation of a meal (right) at a USAID- supported repatriation and return center near San Pedro Sula, Honduras.

Figure 4. Assistance Provided at Reception and Repatriation Center in Honduras.

Efforts to Strengthen Migrant Return and Repatriation Centers

USAID and State have an interagency agreement to provide assistance to strengthen migrant reception and repatriation efforts in all three countries. Efforts under this program have included providing immediate, basic assistance to returnees (see figure 4); undertaking construction efforts to expand and improve existing facilities; and working with host governments to systemize data gathered from the returned migrants. According to officials from the International Organization for Migration, an intergovernmental organization that is implementing the program, this improved data collection should enable better long-term tracking of migrants—including the causes of their migration—and their ability to return to and reintegrate with their communities of origin.

Agencies' Long-standing Efforts Have Sought to Address Persistent Conditions Identified as Contributors to Migration

USAID, State, IAF, and MCC programs have long sought to address what officials have identified as underlying causes of migration, including persistent development challenges such as violence, poverty, and lack of educational opportunities. For example, USAID's Country Development Cooperation Strategies (CDCS) for each country identify citizen security and economic growth as strategic objectives. The agency supports programs in each country seeking to reduce violence, improve economic opportunities through improved agricultural practices and other efforts, and increase access to education and health services, among others. For example, the USAID crime and violence prevention project in El Salvador, which focuses on expanding community-based crime and violence prevention efforts and supporting the government of El Salvador's National Strategy on Violence prevention, includes capacity building for municipalities to prevent violence and establishes outreach centers for youth and children. The agency also supports similar efforts in Guatemala and Honduras (see figure 5).

State has supported programs in each of the three countries we reviewed seeking to reduce violence and improve citizen security by offering training and technical support to prosecutors, the police, and border patrol units, among others (see figure 6). For example, in Honduras, State officials at the U.S embassy described justice sector capacity-building efforts including strengthening host government judicial personnel's ability to develop cases against criminal organizations and other efforts. This includes support for DOJ advisors in Honduras.

Source: GAO. |GAO-15-507

A USAID-sponsored outreach center near Tegucigalpa, Honduras, (left), and an ad inside the center for employment opportunities (right).

Figure 5. U.S. Agency for International Development-Supported Outreach Center in Honduras.

Source: GAO. |GAO-15-507

Trainees at a Guatemalan police academy supported by State's Bureau of International Narcotics and Law Enforcement Affairs (INL) advisors (left); a police surveillance center using equipment donated by State/INL (center); and children participating in a State/INL-supported Police Athletic League (right).

Figure 6. Department of State-Supported Police Programs in Guatemala.

IAF officials said that IAF supports local initiatives in more than 880 communities in El Salvador, Guatemala, and Honduras, with nearly half of its investment in the three countries intended to directly benefit youth through job creation and other community-based activities. For example, IAF provided training and technical assistance to help a farmer's cooperative in El Salvador improve its production and marketing of organic coffee. Finally, MCC's compact in El Salvador and threshold program in Guatemala—each in development prior to the recent migration increase—include programs to improve the quality of secondary education to assist youth in finding employment.[28]

USAID, State, and IAF outlined plans to modify some of these longstanding efforts in response to the rise in UAC migration. For example, in Guatemala, USAID outlined plans to increasingly target youth at risk of migration through various programs and to introduce agricultural programming, including coffee rust-resistant seedlings, and to provide nonagricultural economic opportunities for youth. State and DHS have outlined plans to strengthen border security efforts through their vetted units to stem migration, and to increase the size of antigang units in an effort to reduce violence. In addition, USAID, State, and IAF have each outlined plans to expand various programs to additional communities identified as having high levels of UAC migration. These efforts are discussed in more detail later in the report.

Agencies Have Aligned Program Locations with Long- Term Strategic Objectives and Made Some Adjustments to Reach More Communities Affected by UAC Migration

Agencies have generally located programs in alignment with long-term objectives for El Salvador, Guatemala, and Honduras, such as addressing areas of high poverty and violence. In response to the rapid increase in UAC migration to the United States, agency officials said that they reviewed program locations and determined that most programs were already located in areas that had experienced high levels of UAC out-migration. However, officials also indicated that they have made some adjustments and plan to locate more programs in communities with high levels of UAC migration.

Agencies Generally Aligned Program Locations with Long-Term Strategic Objectives

Most of the agencies in our review have established development objectives for Central America, some of which predate the rapid increase in UAC migration. These objectives are outlined in various strategy and planning documents. In some cases, the development objectives outline priority geographic locations for programs that agencies have identified as addressing underlying causes of UAC migration, such as crime and poverty.[29] USAID's CDCS documents, for example, outline development objectives for each country that focus on specific locations. For example, in Honduras, the CDCS contains two development objectives. The first development objective seeks to increase citizen security for vulnerable populations in high-density urban areas with high crime rates, and specifies two cities—Tegucigalpa and San Pedro Sula—and municipalities in an area referred to as the Northern Corridor as the geographic focus.[30] The second development objective, to reduce extreme poverty in western Honduras, specifies the six western departments, which all have severe rates of poverty and undernutrition, as the focus of programming. Similarly, the CDCS for Guatemala, which contains an overarching goal of developing a more secure Guatemala that fosters greater socioeconomic development in the Western Highlands and sustainably manages its natural resources, states that the majority of USAID resources will be allocated to programming in the Western Highlands, while USAID officials noted most of the remainder was dedicated to security efforts in urban areas. In El Salvador, where USAID aims to increase citizen security, rule of law, and economic opportunity, the CDCS states that the government of El Salvador has identified 54 of 262 municipalities as "high crime," where USAID will focus its crime prevention and education activities.

State country planning documents similarly highlight strategic priorities for the three countries, and in some cases outline priority geographic locations. State Integrated Country Strategy documents, which are multi- year mission planning documents, outline strategic priorities, but do not specify geographic locations to the same extent as USAID's CDCS documents. State/INL's country plans indicate that they are aligned with U.S strategies. In addition, these plans outline various program areas and goals associated with these program areas. The plans specify priority geographic locations for some programs associated with these program area goals. For example, in support of the INL goal in El Salvador of building the government's ability to mitigate the influence of gangs and improve citizen security, the INL country plan outlines plans to launch the Model Police Precinct program in Quetaltepeque, Sonsonate, San Martin, Antiguo Cuscatlan, and La Libertad.

MCC and IAF documents do not outline specific geographic priorities for programs in the three countries, but MCC and IAF officials offered examples of factors the agencies consider in determining where to locate programs.[31] For example, according to IAF officials, IAF awards its grants to grassroots and community-based groups in communities with economic and social disadvantages, often with a history of and increased risk for migration. Geographic location is considered one element of the selection strategy for each country. Also, according to an MCC official in El Salvador, as part of a full-time inclusive school approach, the program may invest in science labs in certain schools in order for other schools in the vicinity to also access them.

Agencies Determined Many Programs Were Already Located in UAC Communities of Origin

Agency officials told us they drew on various sources of information to understand which areas in El Salvador, Guatemala, and Honduras had high levels of UAC migration. In particular, they told us a key point of reference was a DHS-produced map that showed the number of UAC by location of origin based upon Border Patrol apprehension data from January 1 to May 15, 2014. We previously reported that agency officials used this map and DHS data on UAC locations of origin, along with other sources of information, to understand underlying causes of UAC migration and inform programming decisions.[32] During our fieldwork for this review, agency officials provided similar responses, noting that they used this map and DHS data to understand UAC origins or to cross- reference data on UAC origins derived from other sources of information produced by entities such as the International Organization for Migration, USAID's Office of Transition Initiatives, host government agencies, and other local organizations.[33]

Agency officials told us that while the DHS-produced map may have limitations, they believed it to be generally accurate. As we previously reported, CBP officials identified various challenges to obtaining UAC location information, including the inability of children to accurately relay information on their origins, lack of documentation, and inability of border agents interacting with children to collect or record their information accurately.[34] State/INL officials in El Salvador, in particular, stated they did not believe that current available data on UAC origins were reliable as a basis for locating programs as some INL staff who have previously worked in the border regions believe that UAC provide false information because they are concerned about being traced back to their communities. In addition, some agency officials stated that the DHS map lacked specificity or detail, such as identifying neighborhoods associated with high UAC migration within the major cities. Nonetheless, USAID and State officials in the three countries told us that the top UAC locations of origin identified in the map were generally consistent, with a few exceptions, with their understanding of the top UAC locations of origin.

Further, agency officials stated that their established programs were already located in these areas. In Honduras, where over half of the DHS-identified top 20 municipalities in terms of UAC locations of origin are situated, agency officials told us the DHS map confirmed for them that programs already existed in those locations. In Guatemala, USAID and State officials said that they consulted the DHS map and other available information about UAC origin locations and determined that there was a general overlap between those locations and agency programs. USAID officials in Guatemala noted that about 60 percent of the agency's resources in Guatemala are used for activities in the Western Highlands, which these officials said they have identified as the primary area of UAC migration in that country. In El Salvador, USAID officials stated that, according to their review of the DHS map, their programs were already located in areas of high UAC migration. Finally, according to IAF, the DHS map illustrated a general overlap between the location of its grantees and locations with high levels of UAC migration.

We obtained information on the location of USAID and State/INL-funded programs in El Salvador, Guatemala, and Honduras; the location of IAF grantees in these countries; and the top UAC locations of origin in each country, as identified by DHS. Figure 7 shows the number of UAC apprehended by U.S. Border Patrol between January and May 15, 2014, by location of origin in each department across the three countries. Figure 8 shows the total the number of State and USAID programs and IAF grantees in each department across the three countries. See appendix III for figures that disaggregate the number of program locations by country and by agency.

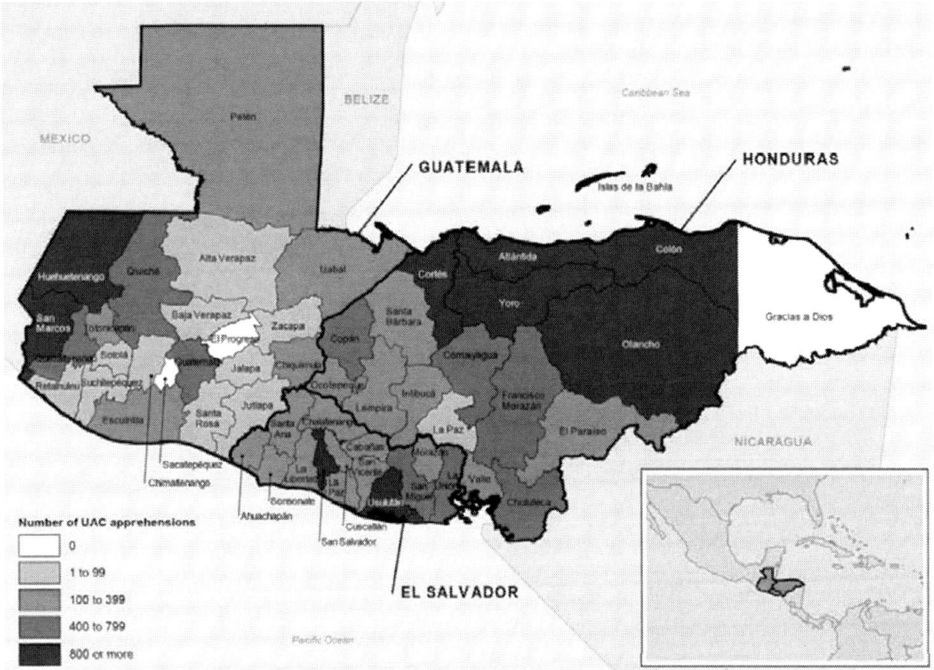

Source: GAO analysis of Department of Homeland Security data. Mapinfo (maps). | GAO-15-507

Note: Data reflect aggregated totals at the department level of UAC by municipality of origin.

Figure 7. Number of Apprehended Unaccompanied Alien Children (UAC) between January and May 15, 2014, by Location of Origin, in El Salvador, Guatemala, and Honduras.

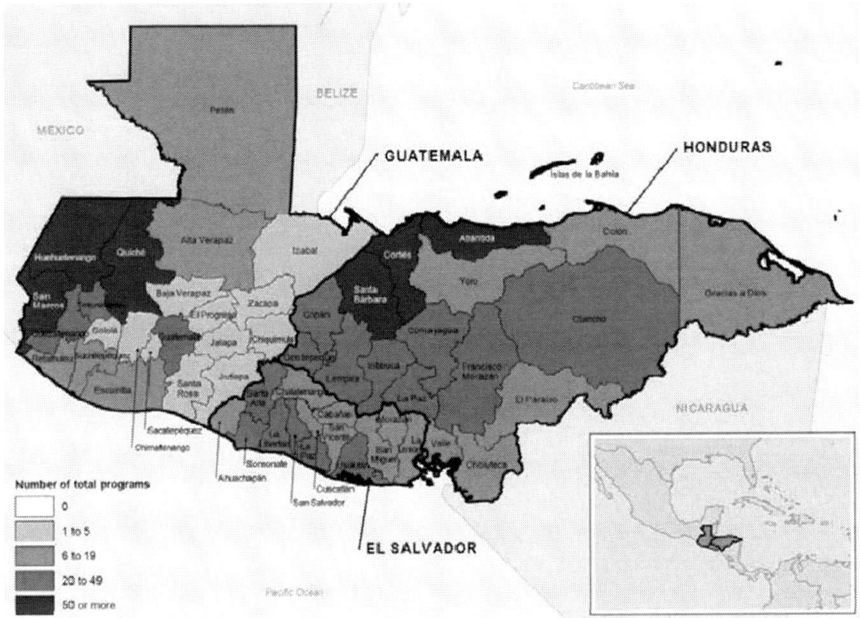

Source: GAO analysis of Department of State, U.S. Agency for International Development, and Inter-American Foundation data; Mapinfo (maps). | GAO-15-507

Note: Data reflect aggregated totals at the department level of U.S. Agency for International Development and State International Narcotics and Law Enforcement Affairs programs and Inter- American Foundation grantees by municipality.

Figure 8. Number of Department of State and U.S. Agency for International Development Programs and Inter-American Foundation Grantees in El Salvador, Guatemala, and Honduras.

Agencies Plan to Locate More Programs in Communities Affected by High Levels of UAC Migration

Agencies have outlined plans and taken some steps in the three countries since the recent rise in UAC migration by adding or expanding activities in locations identified as having high levels of UAC migration. For example, according to State/INL's current country plan for Honduras, State plans to expand violence prevention programs, such as the Gang Resistance Education and Training Program, to reach three new police metropolitan areas in Tegucigalpa and six police metropolitan areas in San Pedro Sula, two areas in the country agencies have identified as having among the highest levels of UAC migration. In El Salvador, USAID outlined plans to expand educational opportunities to youth in additional municipalities with high levels of migration. For example, the Adopt-A-School program, which aims to support the efforts of the private sector, individuals, or institutions who wish to provide financial and other support to schools, has already been extended and expanded to reach additional beneficiaries, including those in municipalities with high numbers of UAC who have been repatriated to their communities of origin. In Guatemala, USAID has outlined plans to expand citizen security efforts to areas outside Guatemala City with high levels of violence and UAC migration, and to expand crime prevention programs to departments in the Western Highlands affected by high levels of migration. USAID has also outlined planned programs that would target agriculture and small business development activities to departments in the Western Highlands with high migration levels. In addition, State/INL has outlined plans to expand municipal policing efforts to the Western Highlands in response to high levels of out-migration from those communities. Also, according to IAF officials, IAF issued grants to several organizations in recent years to support projects in migrant-sending communities or to address migrant issues. As of June 2015, IAF officials indicated IAF had identified at least 19 new programs and 14 modified programs in El Salvador, Guatemala, and Honduras that will seek to address underlying causes of migration in areas with high levels of UAC migration.

However, agency officials also noted the importance of other factors in locating programs. Agency officials suggested that long-term strategic objectives, such as promoting economic growth and social development, remain the focus of their work as they create and locate programs. Moreover, other agency responses to the rise in UAC migration have sought to address UAC migration but have not necessarily been located in areas of high UAC migration. For example, efforts to rehabilitate repatriation centers are located near borders or transit points; legal technical assistance seeks to strengthen government institutional capacity to combat smuggling; countersmuggling operations target key migration routes; and public information campaign activities, such as radio, television, and social media placements do not necessarily target areas associated with high UAC migration.

Most Agencies Have Some Evaluation Processes in Place, but Weaknesses Exist in Performance Measurement of Some Antismuggling Programs

Most agencies have established evaluation processes to measure progress of programs identified as addressing causes of UAC migration. Agency processes to evaluate program effectiveness vary in approach, though DHS and State have not always obtained timely feedback on information campaigns intended to reduce migration, making it difficult to know the effectiveness of these efforts. Agencies have outlined challenges to and approaches for sustaining programs that seek to address the causes of UAC migration.

Most Agencies Have Processes in Place to Measure Progress of Efforts Intended to Address Causes of UAC Migration

Most agencies we reviewed have processes in place to track the progress of programs they have identified as addressing causes of UAC migration. However, DHS has not established performance targets against which to measure units that combat child smuggling, making it difficult to track the progress of these efforts.

USAID and State Use Both Shared and Agency-Specific Mechanisms to Guide Performance Measurement

USAID has developed several documents to assist its missions in developing and managing monitoring and evaluation efforts, which include guidance on establishing performance indicators, baselines, and targets, and on planning and managing evaluations. USAID missions also articulate monitoring and evaluation plans through other key documents, including CDCS documents and Performance Management Plans (PMP). The three countries' CDCS documents also outline illustrative evaluation questions, which can be used to guide long-term program evaluations.[35]

Table 1 provides examples of CDCS development objectives, performance indicators, and evaluation questions for El Salvador, Guatemala, and Honduras.

Table 1. Examples of U.S. Agency for International Development (USAID) Country Development Cooperation Strategy Development Objectives, Performance Indicators, and Evaluation Questions for El Salvador, Guatemala, and Honduras

Country	Development objectives	Performance indicators	Evaluation questions
El Salvador	Citizen security and rule of law in targeted areas improved.	Incidence of selected violent crimes in targeted municipalities. Number of municipalities implementing community policing programs.	To what extent did program activities increase equitable access to educational opportunities for participating in-school and out-of-school youth in targeted municipalities?
Guatemala	Improved levels of economic growth and social development in the Western Highlands.	Prevalence of poverty in target regions. Percentage of underweight children less than 5 years old in targeted areas.	What are the elements that need to be incorporated into income generating activities to achieve a reduction of malnutrition rates in targeted communities?
Honduras	Citizen security increased for vulnerable populations in urban, high crime areas.	Percentage of at-risk youth who express an ability to deflect a life of crime. Secondary school (grades 7 to 9) access rate.	Have there been changes in perceptions of violence indicating that communities feel safer?

Source: GAO analysis of USAID data. | GAO 15-707

Mission PMPs outline monitoring and evaluation plans—including performance indicators, baseline data, and performance targets—to assess progress toward the achievement of CDCS goals. USAID established a PMP for Guatemala that was approved, according to the agency, in October 2013, covering fiscal years 2012 through 2016, which outlines targets by performance indicator by fiscal year for each development objective. For example, for the mission goal of improving levels of economic growth and social development in the Western Highlands, one performance indicator is the prevalence of stunted children under 5 years of age in target regions, with, according to USAID officials, a goal of 63 percent in fiscal year 2013 and 54 percent in fiscal year 2017. USAID anticipates the PMP for El Salvador will be completed in October 2015, and the PMP for Honduras will be completed by late summer 2015.

State's INL bureau uses several documents to guide performance planning and country-specific measurement of programs it has identified as addressing causes of UAC migration. In 2013, State/INL developed several documents to assist INL personnel with designing, monitoring, and evaluating programs. INL country plans for these three countries outline priority areas for INL programs in each country as well as metrics for evaluation under these areas. These documents outline selected activities, indicators, and performance targets for the three countries across each INL program area. For example, the INL plan for El Salvador outlines an objective of establishing model police precincts, with performance targets such as establishing eight new model police precincts within 2 years, and with homicides decreased by 10 percent in these new model police precincts within 4 years. The INL plan for Honduras outlines an objective of embedding a resident legal advisor to improve case management capacity for complex crimes involving human trafficking, with performance targets such as prosecutors increasing their rate of case closure in each of the first 2 years.

State and USAID use various reporting mechanisms to monitor the progress of activities identified as addressing causes of UAC migration. Both State and USAID use State's Bureau of Western Hemisphere Affairs (WHA) annual Performance Plan and Report (PPR) to track the performance of CARSI activities. The fiscal year 2013 WHA PPR, which was the most recent PPR available at the time of our review, provides information on USAID and State performance outputs against established targets. The WHA PPR provides some mission-specific performance information, but generally measures progress at an aggregated regional level.[36] USAID and State also receive progress reports, such as weekly and quarterly reports, that track outputs, activities, and accomplishments during the reporting period. For example, weekly reports on State/INL- funded efforts to strengthen the Honduran border patrol provide updated information on activities such as the number of UAC encountered, as well as seizures, arrests, and inspections, with specific information on coyote arrests. INL quarterly CARSI reports provide updated program information on various CARSI efforts.

IAF Has Established Standard Indicators to Measure Programs

IAF has developed an approach, which it refers to as the Grassroots Development Framework, to monitor its efforts, including selecting project-specific performance indicators and progress reporting. At the onset of specific projects, IAF works with grantee partners to select, from a standard set of 41 indicators, a subset of indicators considered most relevant to measuring the project's desired objectives. Indicators cover areas such as how projects provide for basic needs, training, jobs and income, or how they improve organizational culture and capacity, among others. According to IAF officials, IAF works with grantees to ensure they know how each indicator is defined, to establish baseline conditions against which to measure progress, and to assist them in collecting performance data. Grantees are then required, according to IAF officials, to report every 6 months throughout the grant period on their progress against the selected indicators. IAF's office of evaluation verifies and aggregates results reported by grantees for its annual grant results report, which provides information on basic activity outputs, such as the number of beneficiaries receiving better access to health care as a result of a project, as well as on what it refers to as intangible results, such as the number of grantee partners reporting that individuals had improved their self-esteem as a result of the project. IAF outlined many performance indicators that would be used to measure the 17 projects it identified as having been developed or modified in response to the rapid increase in UAC migration in El Salvador, Guatemala, and Honduras. Among the most commonly used indicators for these 17 projects include the acquisition and application of knowledge and skills and the mobilization of resources.

MCC Plans to Develop Project Monitoring and Evaluation Plans for Compacts and Threshold Agreements

MCC has not yet developed monitoring and evaluation plans for its compact with El Salvador or threshold program with Guatemala but expects to do so in the near future. According to MCC's compact with El Salvador, MCC and the Salvadoran entity managing the compact will develop a plan to monitor whether projects are on track to achieve their intended results and evaluate to assess project implementation strategies, provide lessons learned, determine cost-effectiveness, and estimate the compact's impact. The compact also notes that the results of these activities will be made publicly available on MCC's website. According to MCC officials, a monitoring and evaluation plan for the El Salvador compact will be developed 90 days after the compact enters into force.[37] According to MCC officials, MCC plans for the compact to enter into force no later than September 30, 2015. According to MCC officials, MCC expects to develop a monitoring and evaluation plan for its threshold program with Guatemala sometime between September 2015 and March 2016.

DHS Has Not Established Performance Targets against Which to Assess Progress of Transnational Criminal Investigative Units

DHS/ICE has established performance indicators for its TCIUs, but has not established performance targets, making it difficult to track progress of these units' efforts to combat UAC smuggling and other priorities. We have previously reported that performance measurement allows organizations to track progress in achieving their goals and gives managers crucial information to identify gaps in program performance and plan any needed improvements.[38] In addition, according to *Standardsfor Internal Control in the Federal Government*, managers need to compare actual performance against planned or expected results and analyze significant differences.[39] DHS's *Transnational Criminal Investigative Unit Executive Report* provides overviews of TCIU efforts by country, including country-specific priorities. The report also outlines basic performance indicators used to track TCIU success. These measures are divided into three performance categories—enforcement, capacity building, and intelligence—with various types of outputs by category. The report also outlines success stories and enforcement statistics by country, such as the number of arrests and seizures. However, DHS/ICE has not set targets for these performance measures.

A DHS official told us that State/INL, which provides funding for these units, has lead responsibility for measuring their performance. State/INL country plans for all three countries include a performance indicator of the number of unit investigations conducted, and performance targets for the number of investigations conducted within 2 and 4 years. According to DHS/ICE officials, however, DHS was not involved in the development of State/INL's performance indicators and targets related to these units. When asked, DHS officials did not indicate to us why they had not established performance targets to accompany the performance indicators DHS has already outlined in its *Transnational Criminal Investigative Unit Executive Report*. Such targets would enable DHS to compare outputs—such as arrests made, investigations conducted, or foreign counterpart operations—against the pre-established targets, and to better assess TCIU efforts.

Agencies Have Various Evaluation Processes, but DHS and State Have Collected Limited Information on the Impact of Public Information Campaigns

USAID, State, and IAF have established processes to evaluate the effectiveness of their programs. However, DHS and State have not consistently evaluated their information campaigns intended to reduce migration, making it difficult to know the effectiveness of these efforts.

USAID Has Recently Evaluated Several of its Programs Intended to Address Causes of UAC Migration

USAID conducted several recent evaluations of its programs developed before the rapid increase in UAC migration but identified as addressing the causes of migration.[40] These included evaluations of programs addressing crime and violence prevention and workforce development. For example, in July 2014, USAID published an evaluation of a workforce readiness program, which seeks to strengthen the basic workforce competencies of Honduran youth. The study, which was intended to understand the characteristics of youth participating in the program and the extent to which they had improved perceptions of their employability after participating in it, concluded that youth saw significant gains in job- seeking behaviors, soft-skills development, and number of internships obtained. The study also noted more work needed to be done with youth to understand the skills necessary to compete for their desired jobs. In addition, in October 2014, a study requested by USAID evaluating the impact of community-based crime and violence prevention programs in El Salvador, Guatemala, Honduras, and Panama was published. The evaluation, which gauged perceptions over time of crime victimization and citizen security, found that, as a result of USAID's community-based prevention programs, residents feel safer, perceive less crime and fewer murders, and express greater trust in police. The study also found a decline in reported murders and extortions in participating communities across the four countries.

According to a USAID official, the findings from these evaluations inform future programming in several ways. First, USAID used these studies to inform the design of the current CDCS for Honduras, which was approved in December 2014. Second, the official noted that the workforce readiness program assessment led USAID to more systematically pre-assess students before enrolling them in workforce readiness training programs, which has led to improved certification rates among enrollees. The USAID official also noted that the workforce readiness evaluation is assisting the agency in developing a new workforce development activity intended to better link training and employment for at-risk youth. Third, the evaluation of the community-based crime and violence prevention programs led to a broader commitment from USAID to apply community policing principles to improve law enforcement and reduce violence and homicides in Honduras, according to the official.

USAID officials and documents indicate that USAID plans to measure the impact on migration of some future programs. USAID officials in Honduras and Guatemala noted the agency has considered developing indicators that could measure the effect of programs on migration, such as whether a program affected a person's decision to migrate. Two documents for planned USAID projects in Guatemala outline efforts to measure programs' impact on migration. One document, for a proposed youth employment project, notes that the program's failure would be judged when a youth drops out of the program because he or she migrated to the United States, moved, or became involved in criminal activities. Another document for a planned community-level violence reduction project outlines a series of proposed results and performance indicators, including one result of a reduced number of under-aged migration from targeted communities with a related indicator of percentage of households that report having sent under-aged youth to the United States in the last 12 months. USAID officials in El Salvador, however, noted that it would be difficult to measure the impact agency programs have on decisions to migrate, in part because some migrate for purposes of family reunification.

State Has Efforts under Way to Evaluate INL-Funded Programs in El Salvador, Guatemala, and Honduras

State/INL awarded a contract to evaluate all countries under the CARSI program, including programs in El Salvador, Guatemala, and Honduras, which began in September 2014, according to State/INL.[41] According to State/INL, in addition to other oversight mechanisms, this contract will evaluate projects that are designed to address causes of UAC migration. This evaluation, which according to State/INL is scheduled to be completed in September 2016, is expected to examine whether all planned activities are being implemented and on schedule, whether activities are sustainable, what impact the programs have had, and whether programs have led to any unintended consequences, among other things.

IAF Evaluates Projects at Several Points in Time

IAF conducts two types of project evaluations. First, IAF conducts an end-of-project assessment for all projects. According to IAF officials, upon the completion of the grant, IAF conducts a close out visit to assess the extent to which the project's objectives have been achieved. According to IAF officials, for this process the grantee partner compiles a narrative that details the project's design, implementation, results, and expected sustainability and impact, and identifies what worked and what did not and key lessons learned. IAF also compiles summaries of best practices relevant to each project, according to IAF officials. Second, each year IAF evaluates a smaller selection of projects that ended 5 years earlier. According to IAF officials, IAF conducts these evaluations, which it refers to as ex-post assessments, to determine the extent to which projects proved to be sustainable subsequent to IAF's involvement. IAF began conducting ex-post assessments in 2009, according to IAF officials. These evaluations provide information such as project results, sustainability, and lessons learned. According to IAF officials, IAF has thus far conducted two ex-post assessments of projects in El Salvador, including an evaluation of a project intended to strengthen civic engagement and an evaluation of an agricultural assistance project. IAF has also conducted an ex-post assessment of a project to train midwives in Guatemala. IAF has not evaluated a project in Honduras. According to IAF officials, in 2015, IAF plans to evaluate projects with a focus on youth engagement, including two projects in El Salvador and one in Guatemala. IAF expects these evaluations to be available in 2016.

IAF is considering adjusting evaluations in response to the increase in UAC migration. According to IAF officials, IAF is examining whether it could adapt its grassroots development framework to capture migration data, such as by developing a new indicator related to migration. IAF officials also noted that IAF may add questions to focus group sessions— which IAF conducts to obtain qualitative information about programs— about why people decide to migrate from or stay in their home countries.

DHS and State Have Not Consistently Evaluated Public Information Campaigns

DHS has not evaluated all of its public information campaigns intended to reduce migration. As we noted earlier, DHS carried out campaigns in 2013 and 2014 focused on the dangers of migration, and in 2015 to increase awareness of requirements under the President's executive action on immigration. DHS's Assistant Secretary for International Affairs and Chief Diplomatic Officer has referred to these campaigns as essential in combating the misinformation promoted by smuggling organizations, and stated in March 2015 that DHS will continue to support them. DHS ran its 2013 Dangers of the Journey campaign between February and May, a peak migration period that year and in recent years. Specifically, according to UAC apprehension data from DHS's Border Patrol, the months with the most UAC apprehensions between fiscal years 2010 and 2013 were, in order, March, April, and May. In fiscal year 2014 the top four months were, in order, June, May, April, and March.

At the conclusion of the 2013 campaign's first phase, in April 2013, DHS evaluated the campaign, contracting for a survey of 1,800 citizens in El Salvador, Guatemala, and Honduras (600 per country), including an equal mix of youth and parents, to assess the campaign's impact. Among the survey's findings were that 72 percent of youth and adults recalled seeing the campaign and 43 percent recalled the campaign's tagline. The survey results concluded that the campaign was highly credible, as it reinforced information respondents had experienced firsthand. However, according to a DHS/CBP official, CBP reporting and State research indicates individuals in El Salvador, Guatemala, and Honduras give more credence to what they hear from relatives and friends than to what they hear on the radio and television. Despite this reporting, DHS has not conducted any subsequent campaign evaluations. Instead DHS launched its 2014 campaign at the end of June, by which point migration levels had already peaked and reached record levels, as shown in figure 9. Although DHS tracked the total number of campaign spots, it did not evaluate the campaign's effectiveness.

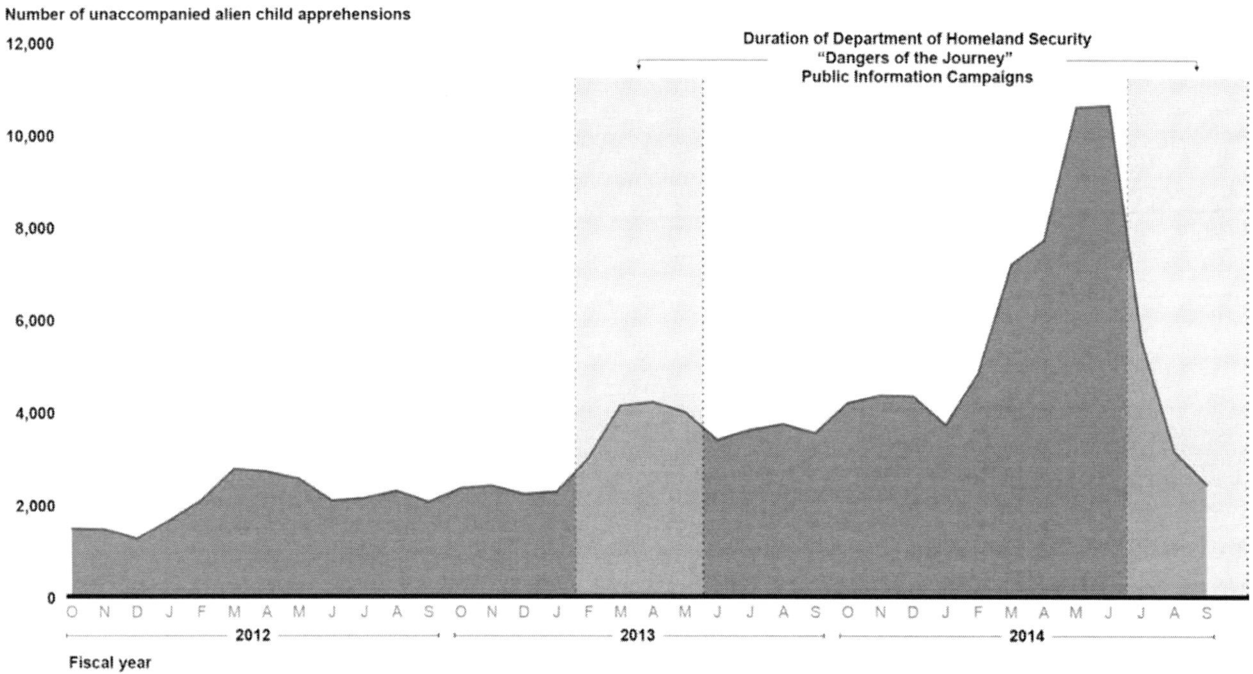

Source: GAO analysis of Department of Homeland Security data. | GAO-15-507

Figure 9. Timing of Department of Homeland Security Information Campaigns and Apprehensions of Unaccompanied Alien Children at the U.S-Mexican Border, Fiscal Years 2012-2014.

A DHS document outlining the 2013 and 2014 campaigns indicates DHS intended to evaluate the second campaign following its conclusion in October 2014. However, an official from DHS's office of public affairs told us that DHS did not conduct the evaluation because of funding constraints. While evaluations certainly add cost, they are an important investment toward ensuring a campaign's success. DHS therefore did not obtain feedback on the effectiveness of its efforts to dissuade migration during a year of record migration levels. Moreover, given that DHS does not currently have an active campaign, and does not plan to launch a new campaign until 2016 at the earliest, as much as 3 years or more may pass between DHS campaign evaluations.

Similarly, while State has collected some information on its public outreach efforts, it has not evaluated the effectiveness of its information campaigns. As we noted earlier, State public affairs offices in all three countries used the DHS campaign materials and developed their own materials to launch related in-country public information campaigns. In Honduras, the public affairs office tracked how many Facebook users the campaigns reached, and how many of these users posted shares, likes, and comments. For example, the office conducted a campaign on Facebook and Twitter to discourage the public from hiring coyotes. According to the embassy's public affairs office, the campaign reached more than 28,000 Facebook users, of which 1,765 posted shares, likes, or comments. In addition, State has conducted in-country focus groups and surveys that have informed some embassy public outreach efforts, particularly concerning the likely impact of certain public messages. However, according to public affairs officers we spoke to in all three countries, State has not evaluated the effectiveness of its actual in- country information campaigns. These public affairs officers told us they did not know what the impact of the campaigns was and believed it would be difficult to measure their impact. One public affairs officer said that the only information available on the campaigns' impact is anecdotal. All three of these officers expressed either uncertainty or doubt concerning the effectiveness of past campaigns centered on the dangers of migration, indicating that it is uncertain whether such campaigns resonated with citizens of the three countries since the dangers were already well known or would not dictate a person's decision to migrate.

As we reported in the past, evaluating information campaigns on a regular basis is a good practice that leading organizations follow, as doing so is considered integral to a campaign's success.[42] Collecting this sort of performance information on media campaigns can provide value in informing future campaign efforts, particularly given DHS's desire to launch a new campaign early next year. Moreover, despite their cost, evaluations are a key investment toward program success.

Agencies Have Outlined Challenges to and Approaches for Sustaining Programs Addressing the Causes of UAC Migration

Agencies have identified various challenges to sustaining programs intended to address the underlying causes of UAC migration. USAID, State, and IAF project documents outline various factors that can hamper the long-term sustainability of projects, such as lack of accountability within government institutions, lack of political will, low tax collection, poor market conditions, and limited private sector engagement. For example, one State/INL country plan notes the host government's limited political will to combat corruption, which is included as a key assumption underlying police professionalization and reform efforts. Similarly, several USAID project documents acknowledge that certain efforts may be only partially sustainable over time because of challenges relating to the host government, such as limited funds or weakened public institutions. In addition, agency officials told us corruption within police and other institutions and extortion against local businesses challenge the sustainability of certain projects.

We observed examples of how some of these factors have the potential to hamper assistance programs. For example, an interagency agreement between State and DOJ outlining efforts to train Honduran prosecutors includes an assumption that the government of Honduras would commit to having a certain number of prosecutors available for at least 18 months to participate in the program. However, at the time of our visit to the country, there were no active prosecutors participating in Tegucigalpa. In El Salvador, where we visited a vocational school that, according to USAID officials, had been established in a joint partnership between USAID and a Salvadoran private company, we observed a computer lab filled with computers recently provided by USAID but with no teacher present. According to USAID officials in El Salvador, the school had asked the Salvadoran Ministry of Education to provide a salary for the teacher, but it had not yet done so at the time of our visit.[43]

Agencies have outlined approaches for seeking to ensure program sustainability despite the challenges described above. State, USAID, IAF, and MCC project documents emphasize the importance of prioritizing improvements to government institutions; identifying sustainable funding sources, such as the private sector; and advocating for legislative and policy reforms that support program objectives. In addition, agency officials have noted the importance of involving communities, the private sector, and the police in program design to ensure they are invested in and supportive of programs' objectives. For example, MCC's compact with El Salvador outlines how MCC assistance over the duration of the compact will decrease to ensure that the government of El Salvador assumes an increasing percentage of related costs. IAF requires that its grantee partners contribute and mobilize their own resources for their projects and, according to IAF, it frequently works with its grantee partners to put in place strategic and financial plans beyond the period of the IAF grant. Some agency performance indicators seek to gauge progress toward meeting sustainability goals, such as by tracking the amount of private funds or other resources invested in community programs in target municipalities, the passage of laws that can facilitate key reforms, and the number of institutions with improved capacity as a result of the program.

CONCLUSION

In recent years, the rapid increase in migration of unaccompanied alien children from Central America has highlighted the crises these children and their families face. U.S. agencies have efforts in place that seek to bring about lasting improvements in these countries and have taken actions with the goal of reducing migration. These actions include DHS's and State's support to Transnational Criminal Investigative Units that seek to disrupt and dismantle smuggling operations and to public information campaigns warning citizens of the dangers of migration and countering misinformation on U.S. immigration policy.

The agencies have limited information, however, on the effectiveness of their efforts to reduce migration. While DHS/ICE has established categories of performance measures for its investigative units, and tracks basic statistical outputs associated with these categories, such as number of arrests, it has not established performance targets that could be used to gauge progress against preestablished goals for these important efforts to combat smugglers.

In addition, DHS and State have collected limited information on the effectiveness of their public information campaigns, with DHS evaluating one of two campaigns and State evaluating none. In not evaluating its 2014 campaign in particular, DHS missed an opportunity to obtain valuable feedback on its efforts to dissuade migration during a year of record migration levels. Because DHS does not have an active campaign, it could go 3 years or longer between campaign evaluations. Such feedback could have offered insight on the effectiveness of past DHS campaign messages, and on their timing, particularly given migration levels had already peaked and reached record highs by the time DHS launched its 2014 Dangers of the Journey campaign in late June. This information would have been particularly valuable in informing any future DHS campaigns. State has conducted research that has informed its public outreach efforts. However, State has not evaluated its campaigns' effectiveness. Timely feedback is critical as campaigns intended to deter migration that is cyclical in nature are time-sensitive. Moreover, given the increased presence of children in recent migration cycles, these campaigns need to be timed right and deliver appropriate messages. Carrying out ineffective campaigns could lead to higher levels of migration to the United States, which is not only potentially costly in terms of U.S. taxpayer resources but costly and dangerous to the migrants and their families.

RECOMMENDATIONS FOR EXECUTIVE ACTION

We recommend the following two actions to strengthen agency performance measurement related to deterring child smuggling. Specifically, we recommend that:

- The Secretaries of State and Homeland Security instruct appropriate agency public affairs officers to integrate evaluation into their planning for, and implementation of, future public information campaigns intended to dissuade migration, such as campaigns warning of the dangers of migration, providing facts on U.S. immigration policy, or conveying other messages. This could include ensuring that available migration data, such as DHS's monthly data on UAC apprehensions, is used to inform the timing of these campaigns, and that the results of campaign evaluations are used to inform future campaigns to enhance their effectiveness.
- The Secretary of Homeland Security instruct DHS's U.S. Immigration and Customs Enforcement to establish annual performance targets associated with the performance measures it has established for its Transnational Criminal Investigative Units.

Agency Comments and Our Evaluation

We provided State, USAID, DHS, IAF, MCC, and DOJ a draft of this report. State, USAID, DHS, and MCC provided written comments on the draft. State concurred with the one recommendation directed to it, and DHS concurred with both recommendations. Specifically, State concurred with our recommendation that DHS and State integrate evaluation into their planning for, and implementation of, future public information campaigns intended to dissuade migration. State noted that it uses a variety of methods to determine the effectiveness and reach of information campaigns and will integrate evaluations into these methods. DHS also concurred with this recommendation and noted that it would consider and evaluate possible markers and metrics of success relevant to each campaign's specific goals and target audiences. In addition, DHS concurred with our recommendation to establish annual performance targets associated with the performance measures it has established for its TCIUs. DHS also noted that it would work with host nation partners to establish goals to measure TCIU investigative activities and capacity development.

State, DHS, IAF, and DOJ provided technical comments, which we have incorporated, as appropriate.

Kimberly Gianopoulos
Director, International Affairs and Trade

Appendix I: Objectives, Scope, and Methodology

In this report, we reviewed (1) U.S. assistance in El Salvador, Guatemala, and Honduras addressing agency-identified causes of unaccompanied alien child (UAC) migration, (2) how agencies have determined where to locate these assistance efforts, and (3) the extent to which agencies have developed processes to assess the effectiveness of programs seeking to address UAC migration.

To address our objectives, we obtained written responses from agency officials identifying programs targeted at addressing agency-identified causes of the rapid increase in UAC migration. We then obtained and analyzed documentation for these programs. To understand broader strategies underlying these programs, we reviewed various strategic and planning documents specific to El Salvador, Guatemala, and Honduras, including the Department of State (State) and U.S. Agency for International Development (USAID) Integrated Country Strategies , USAID Country Development Cooperation Strategies (CDCS), State annual operating plans, and State Bureau of International Narcotics and Law Enforcement Affairs (INL) country plans for each country; the Partnership for Growth El Salvador—United States Joint Country Action Plan; and the Millennium Challenge Corporation (MCC) compact with El Salvador. We also reviewed several interagency strategic and planning documents regarding U.S. engagement with Central America, including the U.S. Strategy for Engagement in Central America, and the U.S. Strategy to Combat Transnational Organized Crime.

We also interviewed U.S. agency officials in Washington, including officials from State, the Departments of Homeland Security (DHS) and Justice (DOJ), USAID, MCC, and the Inter-American Foundation (IAF). We also conducted fieldwork in El Salvador, Guatemala, and Honduras, where we interviewed officials from State, DHS, and USAID in each country, including the ambassadors and deputy chiefs of mission, the USAID mission directors, and DHS country attachés, and met with each embassy's interagency UAC working group. In addition, we met with DOJ officials in El Salvador and Honduras, IAF officials and grantees in El Salvador and Guatemala, and an MCC official in El Salvador. During our fieldwork, we also interviewed representatives from host government agencies in each country, and from nongovernmental organizations in Washington and in El Salvador, Guatemala, and Honduras. We also visited U.S.-funded programs in Central America, including migration reception centers in El Salvador and Honduras. In addition, we met with children in all three countries who discussed their perspectives on causes of UAC migration, experiences, and participation in U.S.-supported programs. Their responses are nongeneralizable.

To address our first objective on U.S. assistance in El Salvador, Guatemala, and Honduras addressing agency-identified causes of UAC migration, we reviewed agency responses to a set of questions we developed concerning what agencies identified as causes of the rapid increase in UAC migration, and agency actions taken in response. In addition, we asked officials we interviewed in Washington and in Central America to discuss the causes of the rapid increase in UAC migration, particularly seeking their perspective on what factors may have changed or emerged in recent years to cause the rapid increase. We reviewed all agency responses to determine the causes agency officials identified. We also asked these officials to discuss agency responses to UAC migration, including programs developed, modified, or planned in response, or programs that predated the increase in migration but that agencies identified as seeking to address underlying causes of migration. We also reviewed agency documents concerning these programs, including project concept papers and appraisal documents, progress-reporting documents including weekly and quarterly reports, and embassy reporting cables, among others. In addition, we obtained funding data from State, USAID, DHS, and IAF on agency funding to El Salvador, Guatemala, and Honduras from fiscal years 2012 through 2014 and funding for specific programs agencies identified as developed or modified in response to the rapid increase in UAC migration. We asked agencies a series of questions on how the funding data were produced, selected, and checked for accuracy, among other things. We determined these data were sufficiently reliable for our purposes.

To address our second objective, on how agencies have determined where to locate programs that seek to address underlying causes of migration, we reviewed agency strategy documents, including those described earlier such as USAID and State country strategies, to determine agency strategic development objectives and, where applicable, priority geographic locations for these objectives. We also reviewed agency strategy and project documents to determine the locations of certain programs developed or modified in response to the rapid increase in UAC migration, including whether such programs were located in areas affected by high levels of UAC migration. We asked agency officials to discuss the factors they considered and prioritized in determining where to locate programs, including programs predating the rapid increase in UAC migration and programs developed in response to the rapid increase in migration, and the extent to which agencies considered communities identified as having high levels of UAC migration in locating such programs. In addition, we asked agency officials how they identified locations with high levels of UAC migration and their perspectives on the accuracy of available information on UAC locations of origin.

We also obtained information, for each country, on the location of UAC communities of origin, of USAID and State/INL programs, and of IAF grantees. In particular, we obtained DHS data on communities DHS identified as having the highest levels of UAC migration between January 1, 2014, and May 15, 2014, for each country. These data included information on UAC locations of origin at the municipal level, and were used by DHS to create a map showing these DHS-identified top UAC locations of origin. DHS officials noted that there were inherent limitations in the accuracy of DHS apprehension data, which we discuss in this report and the report we issued on this subject in February 2015.[44] To assess these data, we had a series of interviews with DHS officials to discuss the process and methodology by which they obtained these data on UAC apprehensions and used them to identify communities with the highest levels of UAC migration and create maps showing these results. We also discussed these DHS data with U.S. agency officials in Washington and Central America. These officials noted they found the DHS data to be generally accurate representations of their understanding of the top UAC locations of origin. Moreover, some of these officials noted that agencies also used the DHS maps in part to determine the extent to which their programs aligned with these top UAC locations of origin. Therefore, we determined that the DHS data on top UAC locations of origin were contextually relevant to the agencies' own understanding of how the locations of their programs aligned with top UAC locations of origin. In order to analyze the locations from the DHS data, we combined the files to create a single master list of locations. We then matched this list to the GeoNet Names Server file from the National Geospatial Intelligence Agency to create a standardized list of names. We then aggregated the locations by department, and presented them in broad ranges. By aggregating these data by department and presenting them in map form in broad ranges, we believe they provide a reliable indication of the relative distribution of UAC-sending locations. We also obtained from USAID and State/INL the locations of all programs in each country, and, from IAF, the locations of IAF grantees in each country. As with the DHS data, we matched this list of programs and grantees to the GeoNet Names Server file from the National Geospatial Intelligence Agency to create a standardized list of names, then aggregated the locations by department, and presented them in broad ranges. We did not include some program locations in our data due to a lack of specificity in agency documents on the locations of certain programs. We provided this information to offer context on the location of UAC communities of origin and of U.S. agency programs and grantees.

To address our third objective, on the extent to which agencies have developed performance indicators to assess the effectiveness of efforts responsive to UAC migration, we reviewed agency documents on programs agencies identified as responsive to the rapid increase in UAC migration, including agency evaluation policies and guides, country strategy and planning documents for each country, monitoring and evaluation plans, standard operating procedures, program evaluations, and quarterly and other progress reports. We also interviewed agency officials in Washington, D.C., and in El

Salvador, Guatemala, and Honduras concerning steps they have taken to monitor and evaluate programs that seek to address causes of UAC migration. We also reviewed *Standards for Internal Control in the Federal Government*, and prior GAO work on performance measurement.[45] In determining the importance of evaluating media campaigns as a good practice that leading organizations follow, we assessed various sources, including federal policies, *Standards for Internal Control in the Federal Government*, prior GAO reports on U.S. public diplomacy, and literature on practices for evaluating media campaigns. These sources outlined the importance of integrating evaluations into media campaigns and noted that while evaluations add cost, they are a worthwhile investment in campaign success.

We conducted this performance audit from September 2014 to July 2015 in accordance with generally accepted government auditing standards. Those standards require that we plan and perform the audit to obtain sufficient, appropriate evidence to provide a reasonable basis for our findings and conclusions based on our audit objectives. We believe that the evidence obtained provides a reasonable basis for our findings and conclusions based on our audit objectives.

APPENDIX II: AGENCY FUNDING TO EL SALVADOR, GUATEMALA, AND HONDURAS OVERALL AND FOR PROGRAMS ADDRESSING CHILD MIGRATION

Agencies we reviewed, including the U.S. Agency for International Development (USAID), the Departments of State (State) and Homeland Security (DHS), and the Inter-American Foundation (IAF), identified overall funding allocated for programs in El Salvador, Guatemala, and Honduras for fiscal years 2012 through 2014 (see table 2). In addition to the funding information provided in table 2, the MCC signed a threshold program agreement with Honduras in fiscal year 2013 totaling $15.6 million, a compact agreement with El Salvador in fiscal year 2014 total $277 million, and a threshold program agreement with Guatemala in fiscal year 2015 totaling $28 million.

Table 2. U.S. Agency for International Development, Department of State, Department of Homeland Security, and Inter- American Foundation Funding Allocated for Programs in El Salvador, Guatemala, and Honduras, Fiscal Years 2012-2014

(Dollars in thousands)				
Country	**2012**	**2013**	**2014**	**Total**
U.S. Agency for International Development[a]				
El Salvador	37,704	35,354	30,631	**103,689**
Guatemala	77,167	73,397	73, 285	**223,849**
Honduras	72,786	67,005	56,700	**196,491**
Department of State[b]				
El Salvador	12,437	12,208	10,207	**34,852**
Guatemala	22,166	15,042	11,249	**48,458**
Honduras	19,048	23,357	18,208	**60,612**
Department of Homeland Security				
El Salvador	1,042	758	1,462	**3,262**
Guatemala	961	1,180	1,176	**3,317**
Honduras	750	515	702	**1,967**
Inter-American Foundation[c]				
El Salvador	2,204	1,693	2,196	**6,094**
Guatemala	2,264	1,544	2,379	**6,187**
Honduras	613	685	2,414	**3,713**

Source: GAO analysis of U.S. Agency for International Development, Department of State, Department of Homeland Security, and Inter-American Foundation data. | GAO-15-707

Notes: Amounts have been rounded to the nearest thousand and therefore may not sum to totals. Data include total amounts allocated by fiscal year.

[a] Data represent funding from the following accounts: Development Assistance, Economic Support Fund, and Global Health Programs.

[b] Data represent funding from the following accounts: International Military Education and Training; Foreign Military Financing; Nonproliferation, Antiterrorism, Demining and Related Programs; International Narcotics Control and Law Enforcement; and Public Diplomacy and Public Affairs. Data do not include Migration and Refugee Assistance funding that was appropriated globally to support arrival assistance for repatriated migrants and other activities. Total funding appropriated globally for this account was $1,200,000 in fiscal year 2012 and $10,311,876 in fiscal year 2014.

[c] Data represent funding from Inter-American Foundation appropriations, the Social Progress Trust Fund, the Inter-American Social Protection Network, and counterpart funding.

Agencies we reviewed also provided funding information on programs they identified as most relevant to addressing unaccompanied alien child (UAC) migration. Specifically, agencies identified programs that were either developed or modified in response to the rapid increase in UAC migration, and provided information on total obligations and disbursements for these programs between fiscal years 2012 and 2014. As is indicated in table 3, State's Bureau of International Narcotics and Law Enforcement noted it was unable to disaggregate UAC-targeted aspects of ongoing funding streams, and instead provided funding information for overall program areas that have been or will be used to address root causes and instances of UAC migration from El Salvador, Guatemala, and Honduras. Funding information for USAID, DHS, and IAF are provided in tables 4 through 6.

Table 3. Department of State Funding for Programs and Program Areas Identified by State as Addressing Unaccompanied Alien Child Migration, Fiscal Years 2012-2014

Country/ program Area	2012	2013	2014	Total
El Salvador				
Improved Border Inspection[a]				
Total obligations	$500,000	0	0	**$500,000**
Disbursements	$272,966	0	0	**$272,966**
Community Policing[a]				
Total obligations	$1,000,000	$1,500,000	$1,500,000	**$4,000,000**
Disbursements	$643,134	$46,312	0	**$689,446**
Criminal Youth Gang Initiative[a]				
Total obligations	$2,365,000	$730,000	0	**$3,095,000**
Disbursements	$406,267	0	0	**$406,267**
Capacity Enhancement[a]				
Total obligations	$3,400,000	$3,000,000	$1,100,000	**$7,500,000**
Disbursements	$923,395	$184,282	0	**$1,107,677**
Partial funding for Government of El Salvador's Public Information Campaign				
Total obligations	N/A[c]	N/A	$140,000	**$140,000**
Disbursements	N/A	N/A	$140,000	**$140,000**
Guatemala[b]				
Improved Border Inspection[a]				
Total obligations	$800,000	$800,000	0	**$1,600,000**
Disbursements	$19,347	0	0	**$19,347.00**
Vetted Units[a]				

Table 3. (Continued)

Country/ program Area	2012	2013	2014	Total
Total obligations	$1,850,000	$500,000	0	**$2,350,000**
Disbursements	$1,489,794	$56,749	0	**$1,546,543**
Regional Maritime and Land Interdiction[a]				
Total obligations	$1,000,000	$1,100,000	0	**$2,100,000**
Disbursements	$103,155	0	0	**$103,155**
Community Policing[a]				
Total obligations	$1,000,000	$1,000,000	0	**$2,000,000**
Disbursements	$179,866	0	0	**$179,866**
Criminal Youth Gang Initiative[a]				
Total obligations	$1,845,000	0	0	**$1,845,000**
Disbursements	0	0	0	**$0**
Capacity Enhancement[a]				
Total obligations	$2,000,000	$1,350,000	0	**$3,350,000**
Disbursements	$70,271	0	0	**$70,271**
Public Outreach Radio Campaigns				
Total obligations	N/A	N/A	$10,000	**$10,000**
Disbursements	N/A	N/A	$10,000	**$10,000**
Public Outreach Newspaper Ads				
Total obligations	N/A	N/A	$14,100	**$14,100**
Disbursements	N/A	N/A	$14,100	**$14,100**
Public Outreach Ads on Public Buses				
Total obligations	N/A	N/A	$21,114	**$21,114**
Disbursements	N/A	N/A	$21,114	**$21,114**
Honduras[b]				
Improved Border Inspection[a]				
Total obligations	$800,000	$1,100,000	0	**$1,900,000**
Disbursements	$433,663	0	0	**$433,663**
Vetted Units[a]				
Total obligations	$2,880,000	$2,000,000	0	**$4,880,000**
Disbursements	$1,553,269	$1,022,546	0	**$2,575,815**
Justice Sector Reform[a]				
Total obligations	0	$1,000,000	0	**$1,000,000**
Disbursements	0	$100,260	0	**$100,260**
Community Policing[a]				
Total obligations	$1,000,000	$1,000,000	0	**$2,000,000**
Disbursements	$311,251	0	0	**$311,251**

Country/ program Area	2012	2013	2014	Total
Criminal Youth Gang Initiative[a]				
Total obligations	$1,840,000	0	0	**$1,840,000**
Disbursements	$221,542	0	0	**$221,542**
Capacity Enhancement[a]				
Total obligations	$11,000,000	$9,300,000	0	**$20,300,000**
Disbursements	$7,146,948	$5,507	0	**$7,152,455**
Protecting Most Vulnerable Youth Often Targeted by Traffickers				
Total obligations	N/A	N/A	$750,000	**$750,000**
Disbursements	N/A	N/A	$750,000	**$750,000**
Regional				
Justice Sector Reform[a]				
Total obligations	$1,500,000	$2,500,000	0	**$4,000,000**
Disbursements	$337,916	$133,800	0	**$471,716**
Capacity Enhancement[a]				
Total obligations	$2,800,000	$4,246,006	$1,000,000	**$8,046,006**
Disbursements	$2,579,444	$3,479,450	0	**$6,058,894**
Mesoamerica Regional Migration Program				
Total obligations	$1,200,000	0	$1,953,376	**$3,153,376**
Disbursements	$1,200,000	0	$1,953,376	**$3,153,376**
Reception and Repatriation Assistance to Returning Families				
Total obligations	N/A	N/A	$7,583,500	**$7,583,500**
Disbursements	N/A	N/A	$7,583,500	**$7,583,500**
United Nations High Commissioner for Refugees				
Total obligations	N/A	N/A	$775,000	**$775,000**
Disbursements	N/A	N/A	$775,000	**$775,000**

Source: GAO analysis of State Department data. | GAO-15-707

[a] Program area identified by State's Bureau of International Narcotics and Law Enforcement Affairs as one that has been or will be used to address root causes and instances of unaccompanied alien child migration (UAC) from El Salvador, Guatemala, and Honduras. The bureau noted it was unable to disaggregate UAC-targeted aspects of ongoing funding streams, and instead provided funding information for overall program areas it identified as most relevant to UAC migration.

[b] According to State's Bureau of International Narcotics and Law Enforcement Affairs, Honduras and Guatemala funds require congressional notification, and fiscal year 2014 funds are on hold for obligation pending congressional consultations.

[c] Not applicable.

Table 4. U.S. Agency for International Development (USAID) Funding for Programs Identified by USAID as Developed or Modified in Response to Increase in Unaccompanied Alien Child Migration, Fiscal Years 2012-2014

Country/program area	2012	2013	2014	Total
El Salvador				
Adopt-a-School Improvements to Public School Infrastructure				
Total obligations	$1,250,000	$577,164	$280,000	**$2,107,164**
Disbursements	$779,253	0	0	**$779,253**
Crime and Violence Prevention Program				
Total obligations	$6,660,983	$2,000,000	0	**$8,660,983**
Disbursements	$3,625,607	0	0	**$3,625,607**
SUPERATE Education and Workforce Readiness				
Total obligations	$410,000	0	$ 500,000	**$910,000**
Disbursements	$324,651	0	0	**$324,651**
Development for Small and Medium Enterprises				
Total obligations	$2,766,870	$2,908,460	0	**$5,675,330**
Disbursements	$2,766,870	$1,890,631	0	**$4,657,501**
Guatemala				
Adjustments to Rural Value Chains				
Total obligations	$6,259,232	$3,029,668	$3,715,526	**$13,004,426**
Disbursements	$3,826,268	0	0	**$3,826.268**
Adjustments to Sanitary and Phytosanitary Standards				
Total obligations	$500,000	$500,000	0	**$1,000,000**
Disbursements	$500,000	0	0	**$500,000**
Adjustments to Cooperative Development Program				
Total obligations	$200,000	$1,091,588	0	**$1,291,588**
Disbursements	$94,085	$613,588	0	**$707,673**
Security and Justice Sector Reform Project				
Total obligations	$7,828,154	$1,290,347	0	**$9,118,501**
Disbursements	$5,932,000	$ 242,035	0	**$6,174,035**
Honduras				
Improving Education for Work, Learning and Success				
Total obligations	$1,250,000	$1,658,852	$4,714,021	**$7,622,873**
Disbursements	$1,830,266	$3,529,296	$3,878,038	**$9,237,600**

Source: GAO analysis of USAID data. | GAO-15-707

Note: Does not include planned programs or programs that have not received funding between fiscal years 2012 and 2014.

Obligation and disbursement totals reflect those for fiscal years 2012-2014 and not necessarily the overall project.

Table 5. Department of Homeland Security (DHS) Funding for Programs and Salaries Identified by DHS as Developed or Modified in Response to Increase in Unaccompanied Alien Child Migration, Fiscal Years 2012-2014

Country/program	2012	2013	2014	Total
El Salvador				
Dangers of the Journey Public Information Campaign				
Total obligations	0	$192,220	$264,799	**$457,019**
Disbursements	0	$192,220	$264,799	**$457,019**
Operation Coyote				
Total obligations	0	0	$50,743	**$50,743**
Disbursements	0	0	$47,655	**$47,655**
Transnational Criminal Investigative Unit				
Total obligations	$460,408	$22,442	$650,097	**$1,132,947**
Disbursements	$460,408	$22,442	$530,774	**$1,013,624**
Guatemala				
Dangers of the Journey Public Information Campaign				
Total obligations	0	$306,226	$456,186	**$762,412**
Disbursements	0	$306,226	$456,186	**$762,412**
Operation Coyote				
Total obligations	0	0	$41,652	**$41,652**
Disbursements	0	0	$31,262	**$31,262**
Transnational Criminal Investigative Unit				
Total obligations	0	0	$675,868	**$675,868**
Disbursements	0	0	$466,001	**$466,001**
Honduras				
Dangers of the Journey Public Information Campaign				
Total obligations	0	$118,451	$214,660	**$333,111**
Disbursements	0	$118,451	$214,660	**$333,111**
Operation Coyote				
Total obligations	0	0	$47,050	**$47,050**
Disbursements	0	0	$37,050	**$37,050**
Transnational Criminal Investigative Unit				
Total obligations	$183,200	$18,265	$432,615	**$634,080**
Disbursements	$183,200	$18,265	$419,528	**$620,993**

Source: GAO analysis of DHS data. | GAO-15-707

Table 6. Inter-American Foundation (IAF) Funding for Programs Identified by IAF as Developed or Modified in Response to Increase in Unaccompanied Alien Child Migration, Fiscal Years 2012-2014

Country/grantee (project description)	2012	2013	2014	Total[a]
El Salvador				
Instituto Salvadoreño del Migrante (Migrant Reintegration)				
Total obligations	0	0	$49,740	**$49,740**
Disbursements	0	0	$24,168	**$24,168**
Museo de la Palabra y la Imagen (Migration, Women, and Environmental Issues)				
Total obligations	0	0	$300,805	**$300,805**
Disbursements	0	0	0[b]	**$0**
Asociación de Desarrollo Comunal Milagro de Dios (Crop Diversification)				
Total obligations	0	0	$33,550[c]	**$33,550**
Disbursements	0	0	$16,126	**$16,126**
Fundación Red de Sobrevivientes y Personas con Discapacidad (Assistance to Disabled Salvadorans)				
Total obligations	0	0	$321,510	**$321,510**
Disbursements	0	0	$91,490	**$91,490**
Sociedad Cooperativa Marías Noventa y Tres (Assistance to Coffee Cooperative)				
Total obligations	0	0	$130,000[c]	**$130,000**
Disbursements[d]	$10,000	$9,148	$81,850[c]	**$100,998**
Asociación Pro-Búsqueda de Niñas y Niños Desaparecidos (Employment and Vocational Training)				
Total obligations	$27,895	$256,085	$41,560	**$325,540**
Disbursements[d]	$58,094	$106,355	$68,956	**$233,405**
Fundación para la Educación Social, Económico y Cultural (Assistance to Microbusinesses)				
Total obligations	0	0	$255,000[e]	**$255,000**
Disbursements[d]	$211,554	$45,636	$138,528	**$395,718**
Instituto para el Rescate Ancestral Indígena Salvadoreño (Assistance Marketing Traditional Crafts)				
Total obligations	0	0	$34,955	**$34,955**
Disbursements[d]	$53,901	$106,161	$51,561	**$211,623**
Guatemala				
Asociación SemillaNueva (Agricultural Assistance)				
Total obligations	0	0	$272,500[f]	**$272,500**
Disbursements	0	0	$34,249	**$34,249**

Country/grantee (project description)	2012	2013	2014	Total[a]
Coordinadora de Asociaciones Campesinas Agropecuarias de Petén (Crop Diversification)				
Total obligations	0	0	$161,210[f]	**$161,210**
Disbursements	0	0	0[b]	**$0**
Asociación Rxiin Tnamet (Expansion of Clinic)				
Total obligations	0	0	$25,985	**$25,985**
Disbursements	0	0	0[b]	**$0**
Fundación ProPetén (Technical Assistance Growing and Selling Coffee)				
Total obligations	0	0	$119,535[e]	**$119,5352**
Disbursements[d]	$180,775	$35,633	$15,847	**$232,255**
Honduras				
Asociación de Desarrollo Pespirense(Support to Youth Microenterprises)				
Total obligations	0	0	$250,000f	**$250,000**
Disbursements	0	0	0[b]	**$0**
Asociación de Desarrollo Triunfeña (Support to Youth Microenterprises)				
Total obligations	0	0	$267,540f	**$267,540**
Disbursements	0	0	0[b]	**$0**
Fundación Hondureña de Ambiente y Desarrollo Vida (Agricultural Assistance)				
Total obligations	0	0	$157,000c	**$157,0001**
Disbursements	0	0	0[b]	**$0**
Vecinos Honduras (Crop Diversification)				
Total obligations	0	0	$133,4502	**$133,4502**
Disbursements	0	0	0[b]	**$0**

Source: GAO analysis of IAF data. | GAO-15-707

Note: IAF obligates grant funds upon approval of each grant. Disbursements are made at 6-month intervals during the period of the grant. Obligations, disbursements, and totals do not include counterpart contributions.

[a] Obligation and disbursement totals reflect those for fiscal years 2012-2014 and not necessarily the overall project.

[b] According to IAF, the first disbursements for this project occurred in fiscal year 2015.

[c] Over 18 months.

[d] These values include disbursements for grants obligated prior to fiscal year 2012 and modified with an award of additional funds during the fiscal year 2012-2014 period.

[e] Over 2 years.

[f] Over 3 years.

Appendix III: Information on Agency Program Locations and Unaccompanied Alien Child Apprehensions by Location of Origin

Figures 10 through 21 provide country-level information on the number of apprehensions of unaccompanied alien children (UAC), by location of origin, as identified by the Department of Homeland Security (DHS) between January and May 15, 2014, and on the number of U.S. Agency for International Development (USAID), Department of State (State) and its Bureau of International Narcotics and Law Enforcement Affairs (INL), and Inter-American Foundation (IAF) programs and grantees in Guatemala, El Salvador, and Honduras. Each agency provided these data by municipality. These figures present these data aggregated at the departmental level. Some locations are not represented in these figures because of a lack of specificity in agency documents regarding the location of the program. Further, the programs were not weighted in any way, such as by number of beneficiaries or population served, or resources allocated to the program location. See appendix I for more information on how we obtained, analyzed, and presented this information.

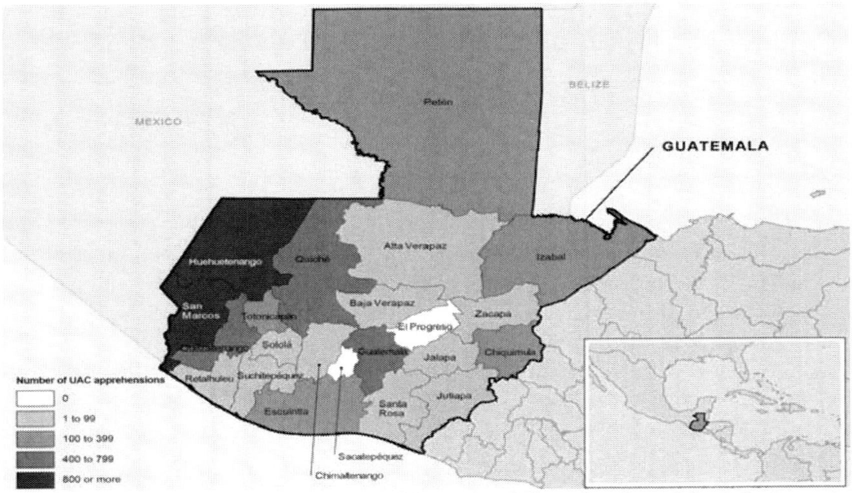

Source: GAO analysis of Department of Homeland Security data; Mapinfo (maps). | GAO-15-507

Figure 10. Number of Apprehended Unaccompanied Alien Children (UAC) between January and May 15, 2014, by Department Location of Origin, in Guatemala.

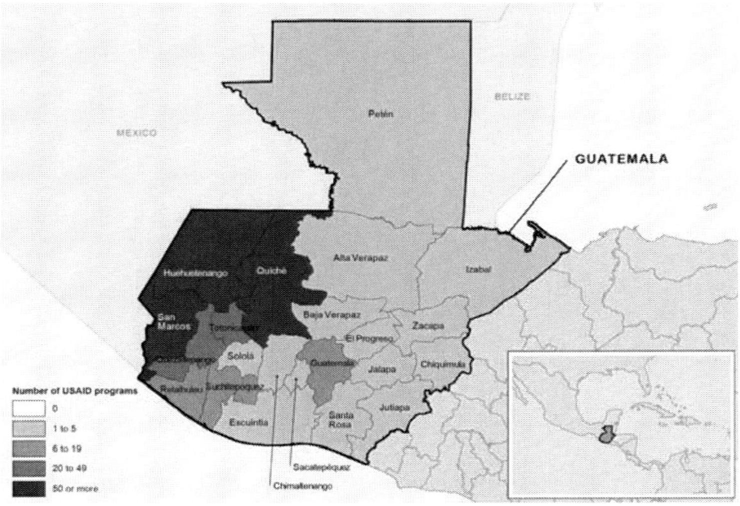

Source: GAO analysis of USAID data; Mapinfo (maps). | GAO-15-707

Figure 11. Number of U.S. Agency for International Development (USAID) Programs, by Department, in Guatemala.

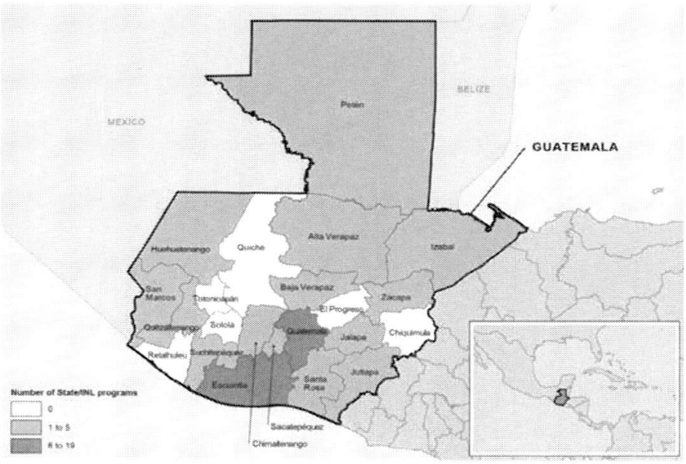

Source: GAO analysis of State data. Mapinfo (maps). | GAO-15-507

Figure 12. Number of Department of State (State) Bureau of International Narcotics and Law Enforcement Affairs (INL) Programs, by Department, in Guatemala.

Source: GAO analysis of IAF data. | GAO-45-707

Figure 13. Number of Inter-American Foundation (IAF) Grantees, by Department, in Guatemala.

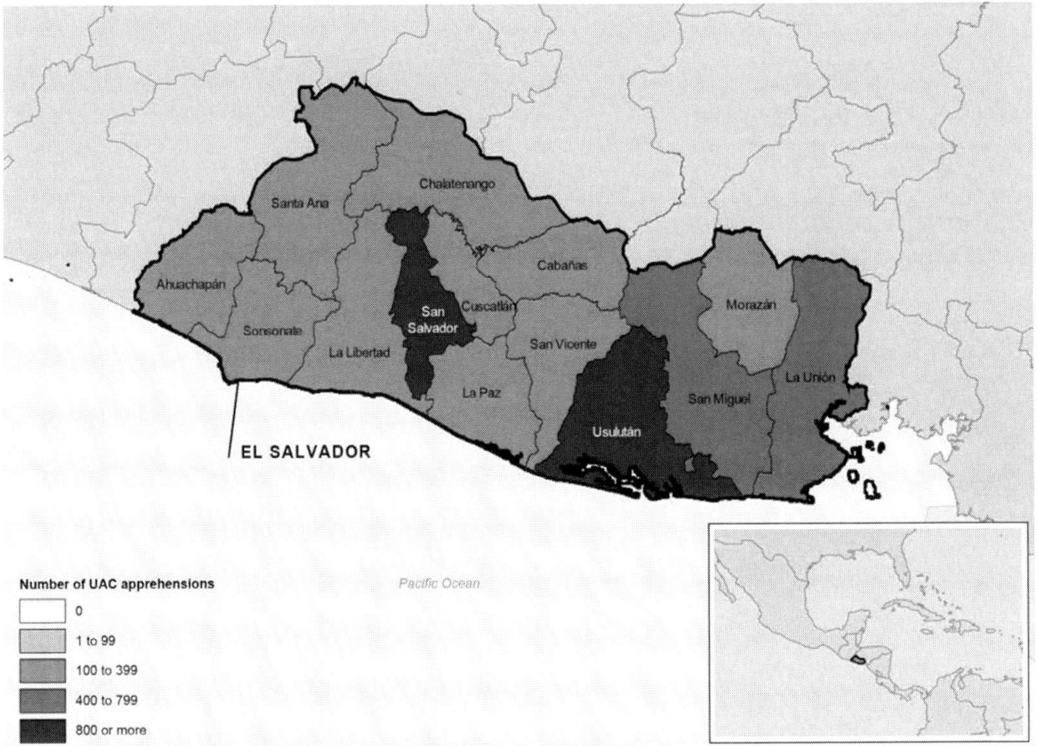

Source: GAO analysis of Department of Homeland Security data. | GAO-15-507

Figure 14. Number of Apprehended Unaccompanied Alien Children (UAC) between January and May 15, 2014, by Department Location of Origin, in El Salvador.

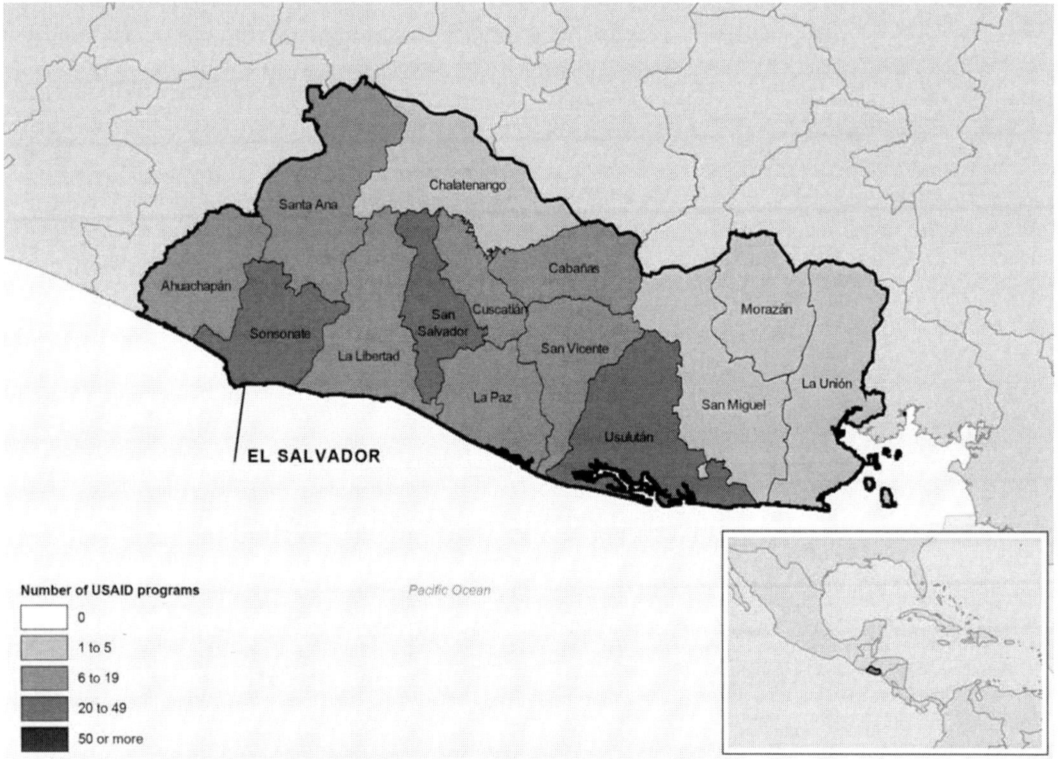

Source: GAO analysis of USAID data. Mapinfo (maps). | GAO-15-707

Figure 15. Number of U.S. Agency for International Development (USAID) Programs, by Department, in El Salvador.

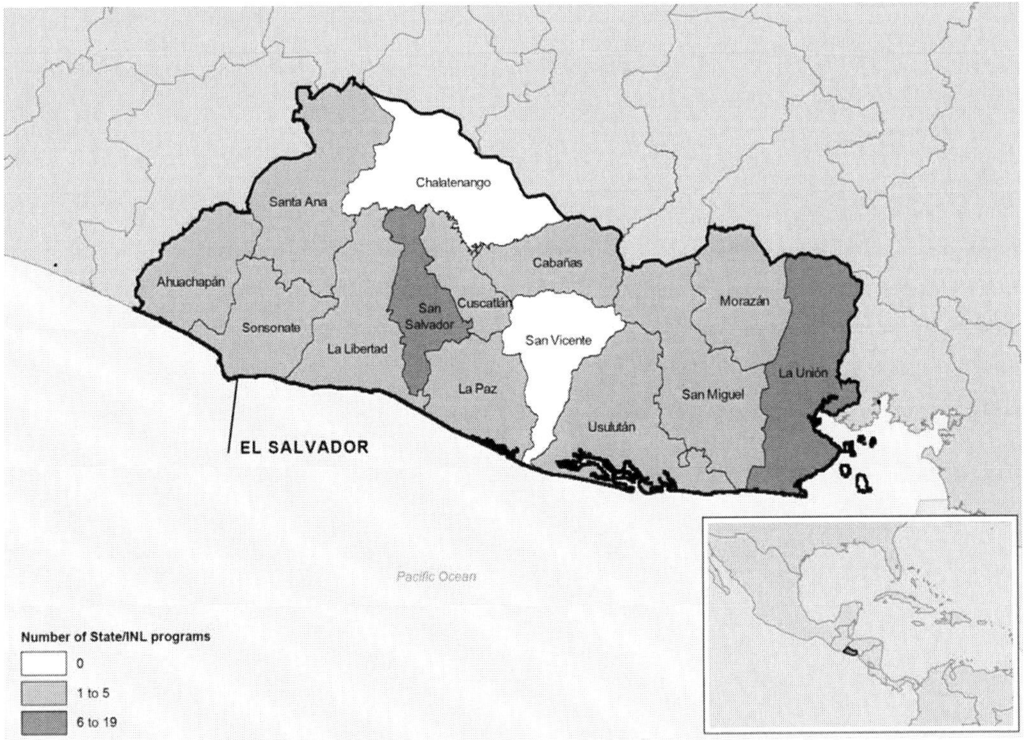

Source: GAO analysis of State data. | GAO-15-507

Figure 16. Number of Department of State (State) Bureau of International Narcotics and Law Enforcement Affairs (INL) Programs, by Department, in El Salvador.

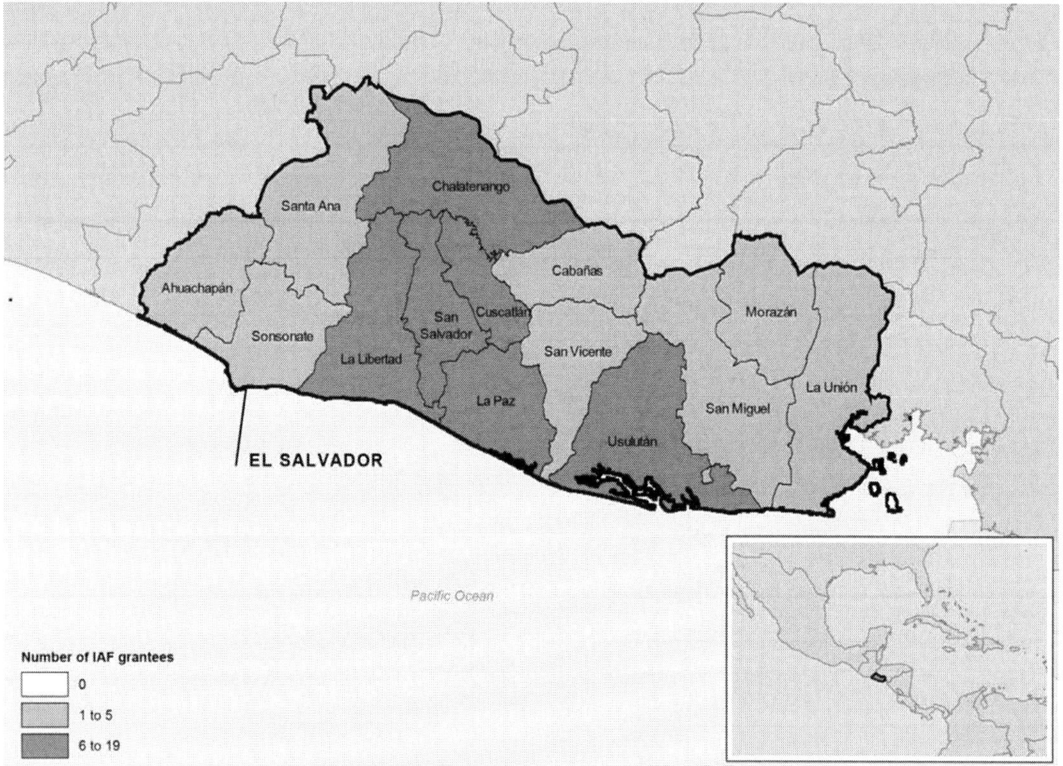

Source: GAO analysis of IAF data. | GAO-15-507

Figure 17. Number of Inter-American Foundation (IAF) Grantees, by Department, in El Salvador.

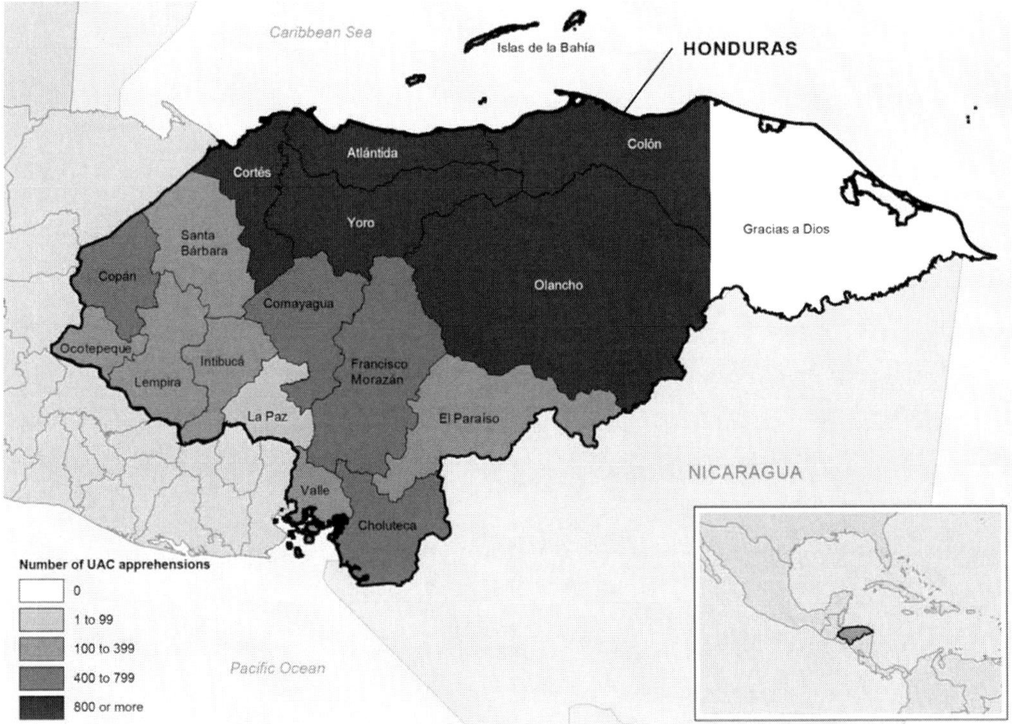

Source: GAO analysis of Department of Homeland Security data. Mapinfo (maps). | GAO-15-507

Figure 18. Number of Apprehended Unaccompanied Alien Children (UAC) between January and May 15, 2014, by Department Location of Origin, in Honduras.

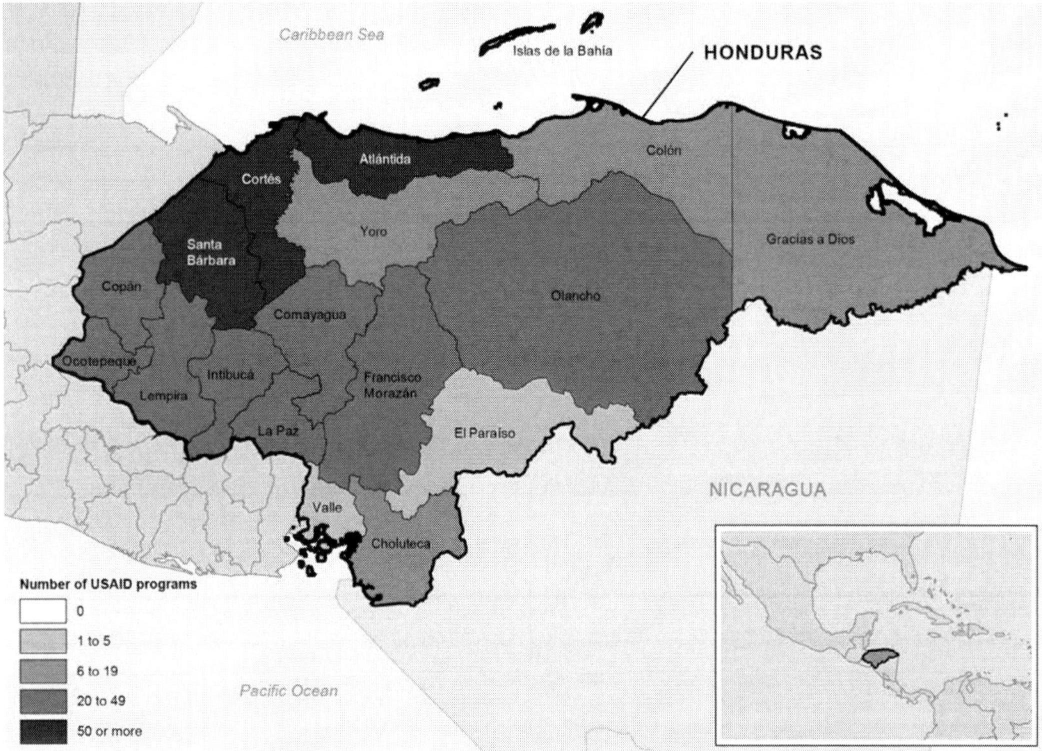

Source: GAO analysis of USAID data. Mapinfo (maps). | GAO-15-707

Figure 19. Number of U.S. Agency for International Development (USAID) Programs, by Department, in Honduras.

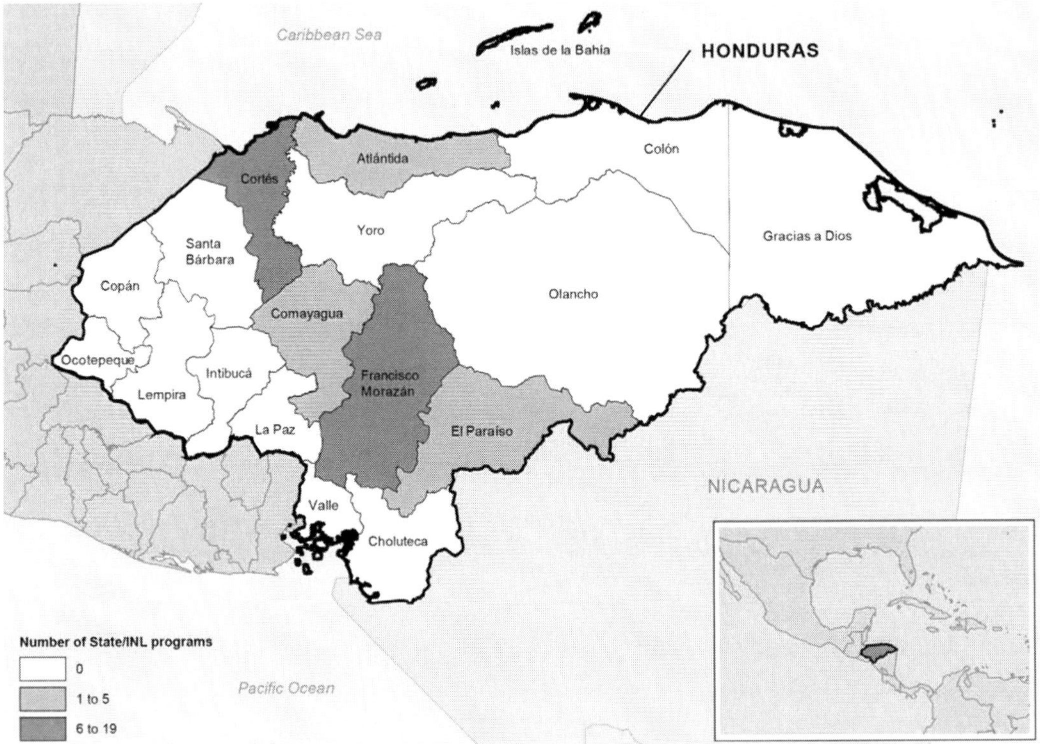

Source: GAO analysis of State data; Mapinfo (maps). | GAO-15-507

Figure 20. Number of Department of State (State) Bureau of International Narcotics and Law Enforcement Affairs (INL) Programs, by Department, in Honduras.

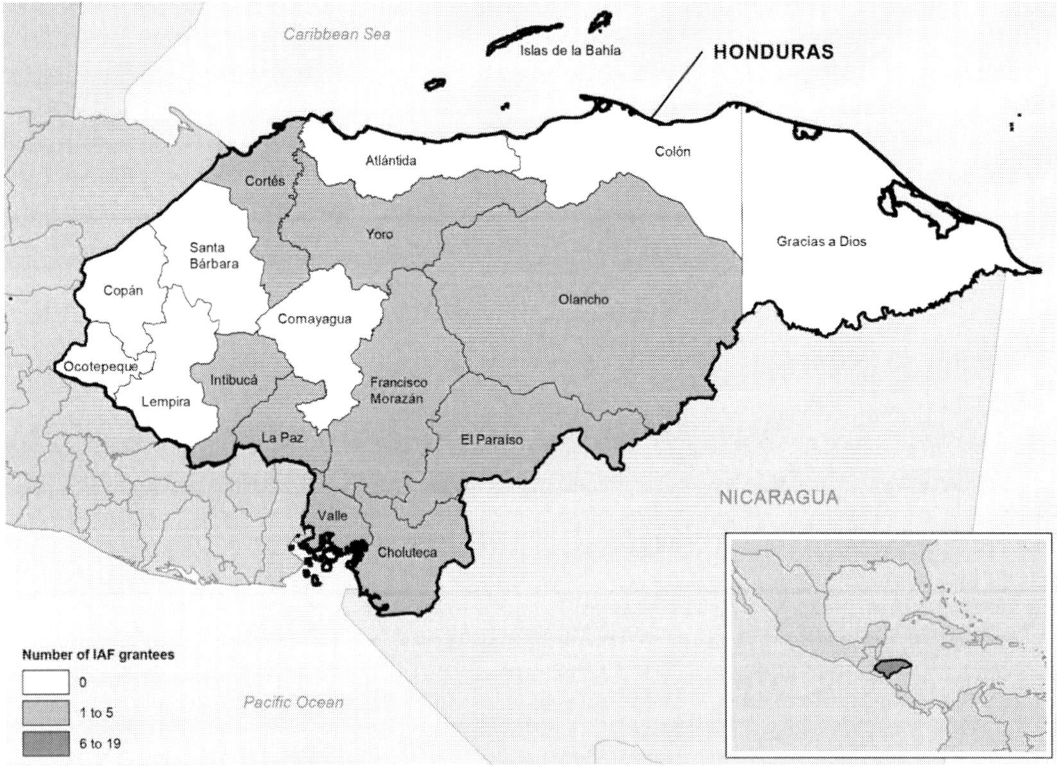

Source: GAO analysis of IAF data. | GAO-15-507

Figure 21. Number of Inter-American Foundation (IAF) Grantees, by by Department, in Honduras.

End Notes

[1] U.S. law defines an unaccompanied alien child, or UAC, as "a child who has no lawful immigration status in the United States; has not attained 18 years of age; and with respect to whom there is no parent or legal guardian in the United States or no parent or legal guardian in the United States available to provide care and physical custody." 6 U.S.C. § 279(g)(2).

[2] GAO, *Central America: Information on Migration of Unaccompanied Children from El Salvador, Guatemala, and Honduras*, GAO-15-362 (Washington, D.C.: Feb. 27, 2015).

[3] MCC was created by Congress in 2004. It forms partnerships with poor countries that have committed to good governance, economic freedom, and investments in their citizens by providing them with large-scale grants to reduce poverty through sustainable economic growth.

[4] IAF, which was created by Congress in 1969, seeks to complement the work of other U.S. agencies in Central America by investing directly in projects that are designed, led, and implemented by the affected communities. According to IAF, it invests only in the most promising proposals it receives and requires grantee partners to contribute significant resources to their projects—on average, $1.3 for every $1 from IAF.

[5] GAO, *Unaccompanied Alien Children: Actions Needed to Ensure Children Receive Required Care in DHS Custody*, GAO-15-521 (Washington, D.C.: July 14, 2015).

[6] Within DHS, CBP and U.S. Immigration and Customs Enforcement (ICE) apprehend, process, temporarily detain, and care for UAC who attempt to illegally enter the United States.

[7] Border Patrol apprehension data for fiscal year 2009 through July 2014 were obtained in August 2014, and data for August and September 2014 were obtained in October 2014. Office of Field Operations apprehension data for fiscal years 2012 and 2013 were queried as of August 2014, and data for fiscal year 2014 were queried as of October 2014. The Office of Field Operations was not able to provide the number of UAC apprehended during fiscal years 2009 through 2011 because it had data only for the number of children apprehended and could not break out how many were UAC and how many were accompanied children. ICE apprehension data for fiscal years 2009 through 2014 were queried as of October 2015.

[8] GAO-15-362.

[9] United Nations Office on Drugs and Crime, *Global Study on Homicide, 2013* (Vienna, March 2014).

[10] United Nations High Commissioner for Refugees, *Children on the Run: Unaccompanied Children Leaving Central America and Mexico and the Need for International Protection* (Washington, D.C.: March 2014).

[11] The Wilson Center, established by Congress, is a non-partisan policy forum, which seeks to address global issues through independent research and dialogue.

[12] Eric Olsen, *How to Address Child Migration from Central America*, Woodrow Wilson International Center for Scholars, (Washington, D.C.: August 2014).

[13] Transparency International is an NGO that monitors corporate and political corruption in international development. The Corruption Perception Index ranks countries around the world according to the degree of corruption that is perceived to exist among public officials and politicians on an annual basis. A lower ranking means a higher degree of corruption is perceived to exist.

[14] *Plan of the Alliance for Prosperity in the Northern Triangle: A Road Map.* Regional Plan Prepared by El Salvador, Guatemala, and Honduras. September 2014.

[15] This includes programs managed by State's Bureaus of International Narcotics and Law Enforcement; Population, Refugees, and Migration; and Western Hemisphere Affairs.

[16] This includes programs managed by DHS's CBP and ICE.

[17] A compact is a multiyear agreement between MCC and an eligible country to fund specific programs targeted at reducing poverty and stimulating economic growth. MCC's threshold program is designed to assist countries that have not yet qualified for compact assistance but

have demonstrated a significant commitment to improving their performance on the corporation's eligibility criteria.

[18] GAO, *Central America: U.S. Agencies Considered Various Factors in Funding Security Activities, but Need to Assess Progress in Achieving Interagency Objectives,* GAO-13-771 (Washington, D.C.: Sept. 25, 2013).

[19] The White House, *Our Central American Strategy* (posted March 16, 2015), accessed July 14, 2015, https://www.whitehouse.gov/blog/2015/03/16/our-central-american- strategy.

[20] San Pedro Sula was named the world's most violent city, outside of war zones, in 2013, according to Consejo Ciudadano para la Seguridad Publica y la Justicia Penal A.C, a Latin American think tank.

[21] Deferred Action for Childhood Arrivals was announced by the Secretary of Homeland Security on June 15, 2012. Certain people already in the United States who came to the United States before they were 16 and meet guidelines established by DHS may request consideration of deferred action, which defers their removal from the United States for a certain period of time. It does not provide lawful status, but recipients are eligible for work authorization.

[22] The Western Highlands are a remote, mountainous area in the western part of Guatemala, inhabited by over 20 different indigenous groups. According to USAID and State officials in Guatemala, this is an area of high UAC migration.

[23] These children do not represent a generalizable sample.

[24] Funding for INL programs is generally provided through the International Narcotics Control and Law Enforcement account. For the most recent appropriation of this account, see Consolidated and Further Continuing Appropriations Act, 2015, Pub. L. No. 113-235, 128 Stat. 2130, 2592.

[25] The federal government's most recent motion to stay the preliminary injunction or narrow its scope pending appeal was denied. See *Texas v. United States*, No. 15-40238, 2015 WL 3386436 (5th Cir., May 26, 2015).

[26] Section 101(a)(42)(B) of the Immigration and Nationality Act defines a refugee, in part, as any person who is within the country of such person's nationality or, in the case of a person having no nationality, within the country in which such person is habitually residing, and who is persecuted or who has a well-founded fear of persecution on account of race, religion, nationality, membership in a particular social group, or political opinion

[27] To qualify for the refugee/parole program, parents must be at least 18 years old and lawfully present in the United States in one of the following categories: permanent resident status, temporary protected status, or withholding of removal; or who have been issued parole or deferred action for a minimum of 1 year. In some cases, the qualifying parent may also apply for other eligible family members, including the in-country parent if that parent lives with the child and is legally married to the qualifying parent in the United States.

[28] MCC officials noted that MCC's current threshold program with Honduras, which aims to improve public financial management and the effectiveness and transparency of public-private partnerships, was not directly relevant to causes of UAC migration.

[29] According to DHS, the department is developing an international engagement strategy, which will include regional priorities for Central America, but not country-level priorities.

[30] The municipalities include Choloma, Tela, and La Ceiba, which are near the northern coast of Honduras.

[31] In September 2012, MCC completed a $461 million compact focused on economic development in the northern zone of El Salvador. In September 2014, MCC signed another $277 million compact with the government of El Salvador. This compact will enter into force once the United States and El Salvador complete certain specified requirements.

[32] GAO-15-362.

[33] Operating within the USAID Bureau for Democracy, Conflict, and Humanitarian Assistance, the Office of Transition Initiatives provides short-term assistance targeted at agency-identified key political transition and stabilization needs.

[34] GAO-15-362.

[35] Guatemala's CDCS covers fiscal years 2012-2016, El Salvador's CDCS covers fiscal years 2013-2017, and Honduras's CDCS covers fiscal years 2015-2019.

[36] We do not provide more detailed information on results discussed in the report because that information is considered "Sensitive but Unclassified."

[37] MCC's compact with El Salvador outlines various requirements the host government must meet before the compact enters into force.

[38] GAO, *Executive Guide: Effectively Implementing the Government Performance and Results Act*, GGD-96-118 (Washington, D.C.: June 1996).

[39] GAO, *Standards for Internal Control in the Federal Government*, GAO/AIMD-00-21.3.1 (Washington, D.C.: November 1999).

[40] USAID's Automated Directives System outlines agency evaluation policies.

[41] The State/INL bureau evaluation plan notes that the State/INL bureau has significantly increased the number of its evaluations since State announced its new program evaluation policy in 2012.

[42] GAO, *U.S. Public Diplomacy: State Department Expands Efforts but Faces Significant Challenges,* GAO-03-951 (Washington, D.C.: September 2003), and *U.S. Public Diplomacy: Actions Needed to Improve strategic Use and Coordination of Research*, GAO-07-904 (Washington, D.C.: July 2007).

[43] Subsequent to our visit, USAID officials in Washington, D.C., noted that while the ministry had not provided the salary for the requested information management teacher, it had provided salary for two other staff that had been requested at the same time, and that the school has drawn on other teachers in an effort to manage the lab and teach basic computer skills.

[44] GAO, *Central America: Information on Migration of Unaccompanied Children from El Salvador, Guatemala, and Honduras*, GAO-15-362 (Washington, D.C.: Feb. 27, 2015).

[45] GAO, *Standards for Internal Control in the Federal Government*, GAO/AIMD-00-21.3.1 (Washington, D.C.: November 1999).

In: Migration of Unaccompanied Children … ISBN: 978-1-63484-604-2
Editor: Angie Hopkins

Chapter 2

OPENING STATEMENT RON JOHNSON, CHAIRMAN, SENATE COMMITTEE ON HOMELAND SECURITY AND GOVERNMENTAL AFFAIRS. HEARING ON "ONGOING MIGRATION FROM CENTRAL AMERICA: AN EXAMINATION OF FISCAL YEAR 2015 APPREHENSIONS"*

Last summer, we witnessed a humanitarian crisis, as more than 51,000 unaccompanied minors from Central America, and almost as many family units, came across the U.S.-Mexico border. Earlier this year, the Committee examined the government's response to this crisis, recognizing that even though the 2015 numbers were lower than 2014, the crisis was far from over as we had not addressed the root cause incentives for unlawful UAC migration.

However, just as the Committee was examining this important topic, apprehensions in the Rio Grande Valley sector in South Texas began to increase. In August, 3,610 unaccompanied minors from Central America were apprehended at the southwest border, up from 2,043 in August 2014—representing a more than 75 percent increase. Representatives from the

---

* This is an edited, reformatted and augmented version of a statement presented October 21, 2015 before the Senate Committee on Homeland Security and Governmental Affairs.

Department of Homeland Security and the State Department have indicated that they expect apprehension numbers to continue to increase this fall.

In the past, apprehensions along the southwest border have been seasonal, with the majority of migrants entering in the spring, largely in response to the agriculture growing season. This year, for the first time ever, this seasonal pattern has changed, as apprehensions did not begin to rise until July. There are several different rationales for this transition. Some observers have suggested that, rather than come to the U.S. to work, migrants are now traveling when their families already in the U.S. send money to reunite with them. Others have rationalized that numbers were down earlier this year due to Mexico's increased enforcement of its southern border but smugglers have finally been able to find their way around these barriers and re-route people to avoid apprehensions in Mexico.

The purpose of this hearing is to assess the causes behind the ongoing migration from Central America, including the recent influx of unaccompanied minors and family units arriving at the southwest border. After this hearing, I will be traveling with several members of the committee to Central America to witness firsthand how both pull and push factors are contributing to this renewed spike in migration from Central America. I encourage all Committee members to join us on this fact-finding trip.

In the meantime, we have an expert panel of witnesses today, many of whom have traveled to Central America themselves, or, work on the frontline at our borders and have personally interviewed those apprehended in South Texas. I thank all of our witnesses for their willingness to share their important experiences and I look forward to their testimony.

In: Migration of Unaccompanied Children … ISBN: 978-1-63484-604-2
Editor: Angie Hopkins

Chapter 3

TESTIMONY OF DR. KEVIN CASAS-ZAMORA, SENIOR FELLOW AND DIRECTOR, PETER D. BELL RULE OF LAW PROGRAM, INTER-AMERICAN DIALOGUE. HEARING ON "ONGOING MIGRATION FROM CENTRAL AMERICA: AN EXAMINATION OF FISCAL YEAR 2015 APPREHENSIONS"*

Over the past five years, slightly over 100,000 unaccompanied migrant children from Guatemala, Honduras and El Salvador have been apprehended at the US southern border. They are but a sub-set –albeit a particularly tragic one—of the approximately three million migrants from the so-called Northern Triangle of Central America that have reached US shores over the past two decades, often after a harrowing journey that could belong in the pages of Dante's *Inferno*.

At the root of this exodus lies a complex brew of structural problems that besets these three small countries. In this mix, factors such as the chronic weakness of the state, the endemic corruption, the glaring economic fragility, and the collapse of public order play decisive roles and reinforce each other. These challenges are unlikely to subside any time soon and will continue to dash the hopes entertained for the region two decades ago, in the wake of the

* This is an edited, reformatted and augmented version of testimony presented October 21, 2015 before the Senate Committee on Homeland Security and Governmental Affairs.

end of civil wars and the emergence of fledgling democratic institutions. More importantly for the purposes of this discussion, these problems are not easily amenable to external solutions. Foreign assistance to Central America's Northern Triangle is useful, even necessary, but will not –irrespective of its generosity—remedy the region's profound development imbalances and institutional shortcomings. Central Americans must accept that, just as only they could put an end to the region's civil conflicts two decades ago they must also take responsibility for building modern states, overhauling law enforcement institutions, and providing opportunities for young people.

The roots of a tragedy. Four factors are at the heart of migration flows from the Northern Triangle and, ultimately, at the heart of the region's travails:

The weakness of the state. The most remarkable feature about states in the Northern Triangle is their extraordinary feebleness by almost any standard. There are many signs of this fragility, but none is more important or far reaching in its effects than the fiscal precariousness of the state in El Salvador, Honduras and, especially, Guatemala. Concerning the tax structure, the situation in the Northern Triangle, as in much of Latin America, is lamentable. At just below 16% of GDP, the average tax burden in Northern Central America is below the Latin American average and stands at less than half the average tax revenue collected by the developed countries of the OECD. The way those taxes are collected is arguably worse – well over half of that revenue is comprised of indirect taxes, i.e. taxes that are unrelated to the wealth of tax payers.

Such fiscal starvation impinges directly on the ability of the state to mitigate the impact of the unacceptably high levels of poverty and inequality that afflict these countries. Poverty affects around two thirds of Hondurans, well over one half of Guatemalans, and 30% of the population of El Salvador. In Honduras, nearly one half of the population lives in extreme deprivation, meaning that they don't even have enough to feed themselves. Moreover, this is a region where the richest 10% of the population is between 18 (El Salvador) and 54 (Honduras) times richer than the poorest 10%. Yet, in Honduras, Guatemala and El Salvador public expenditure on education, healthcare, housing and social security hovers around or barely above $200 per capita per year. In Uruguay it is $1,600. In Finland it is almost $11,000.

The fiscal weakness of states in the Northern Triangle has profound consequences. A society that is unable to do something about deprivation and inequality runs a significant risk of experiencing high levels of violence and a certain kind of politics, where the populist temptation becomes a permanent danger. More fundamentally, fiscally weak states have great problems creating national institutions able to exert effective control over their territory. It is hardly surprising, for instance, that Guatemala, a country that collects barely above 10% of GDP in taxes, faces a peculiarly acute challenge of organized crime. Such a paltry level of tax collection –one of the world's lowest—means, in practice, that state institutions do not travel much beyond urban areas.

Ultimately, the inability of the state to provide adequate public goods and services –including personal safety, the most basic of all public goods—has multiple corrosive effects on democratic stability and development.

Endemic corruption. The deleterious effects of fiscal weakness are compounded in Northern Central America by the presence of widespread corruption, notably in Guatemala and Honduras. The case of *"La Linea"*–the ploy to siphon off custom duties which led to the recent removal from office of Guatemalan President Otto Pérez-Molina—and the embezzlement of over $335 million from Honduras' Social Security Institute, are but recent examples of the corrupt practices that pervade states in the Northern Triangle. These practices are the result of a toxic combination of factors –the blurring of lines between public and private activities by entrenched elites, the growing penetration of organized crime in political structures, the overlapping of political elites and the media, and, above all, the dire state of judicial institutions, which inexorably leads to widespread impunity. The scale of the problem ought not to be underestimated. Relative to the size of the economy, the irregularities uncovered at Honduras' Social Security system –equivalent to nearly 2% of the country's GDP—dwarf the massive bribery scandal at Brazil's Petrobras by a factor of 20.

This is reflected in the poor scores that Guatemala and Honduras receive in every corruption measurement available. In 2014, Guatemala and Honduras stood at the 115th and 126th places out of 175 countries in Transparency International's Corruption Perception Index. Among Latin American countries, only Nicaragua, Paraguay and Venezuela were ranked below. Similarly, the 2014 World Bank's Worldwide Governance Indicators placed Guatemala and Honduras in the percentiles 28 and 23, respectively, in terms of the ability of their institutions to control corruption. Moreover, their scores on this variable have remained static (Guatemala) or deteriorated (Honduras) since 1998. According to the Latin American Public Opinion Project's Americas Barometer 2014, 20.7% of Guatemalans and 23% of Hondurans were asked for a bribe in the previous year. It is important to note that in all these measurements El Salvador tends to score significantly better than its neighbors and closer to the Latin American norm. For instance, it occupied the

80th position in Transparency International's 2014 ranking, trailing only Costa Rica in the Central American region.

As suggested above, the state of judicial institutions is a crucial explanatory factor in this story. In all three countries, political interference in judicial and, more broadly, overseeing institutions (such as the Attorney General, Comptroller's Office, Ombudsman, etc.) is rife, belying in practice the spirit of the legal processes to appoint these authorities and, more generally, the notion of checks and balances. The premature removal from office of greatly respected Attorney General Claudia Paz y Paz by Guatemala's Constitutional Court in 2014, widely seen as politically motivated; the crass dismissal of four members of Honduras' Supreme Court by the National Congress in 2012, a direct retaliation for rulings objected to by the then Speaker of Congress and now President, Juan Orlando Hernández; and the grave political impasse between El Salvador's National Assembly and Supreme Court over the appointment of the members of the latter in 2012, are a few examples of the very limited autonomy enjoyed by the institutions entrusted with enforcing the law and controlling the exercise of power. As the current example of Brazil and, more surprisingly, Guatemala vividly show, the presence of independent prosecutors and judges is an essential component of any effort to eradicate malfeasance and hold politicians accountable. The precarious independence of judges is surely one of the reasons why, according to *Latinobarómetro 2015*, a regional survey, levels of trust in the judiciary in the Northern Triangle are exceptionally low. Only 23% of Guatemalans declare having some or a lot of trust in the judiciary, a figure that falls to 22% in the case of Honduras and 16% in El Salvador, the lowest figure in Latin America.

More broadly, the endemic corruption and the chronic weakness of checks and balances that underlies it are surely two key factors that help explain why El Salvador, Honduras and Guatemala are the three countries at the bottom of Latin America when it comes to levels of support for democracy as a political system. According to *Latinobarómetro 2015*, only 41% of Salvadorans, 40% of Honduras and 33% of Guatemalans prefer democracy to any other government system, well below the Latin American average (56%).

That is why the recent removal from office and arrest of Guatemala's President Otto PérezMolina marks a watershed in the region's history. It offers a glimmer of hope in a region where corruption and impunity have long doomed institutions to sub-par performance. It also suggests that the convergence of an active civil society and external pressure –in this case embodied by the UN-sponsored International Commission against Impunity in

Guatemala (CICIG by its Spanish acronym)—can activate long-dormant accountability mechanisms and checks on power. This is far from sufficient to clean up rotten political systems, but is a crucial step in the right direction. The struggle for democracy and development in Central America's Northern Triangle is, above all, a fight for the rule of law, a battle for accountability and, therefore, against all forms of impunity.

Economic vulnerability. The woeful state of political institutions and the chronic under provision of public goods are accurate predictors of serious economic shortcomings. For the vast majority of migrants from Northern Central America economic reasons underlie the decision to leave their countries. Despite the significant efforts made by all three countries to open up their economies, their economic structures appear unable to generate the kind of growth that could make a real dent in their high levels of poverty and social exclusion. Over the past decade, per capita income growth in Honduras (2.3% on average in 2003-12), El Salvador (1.5%) and, particularly, Guatemala (0.9%) has been mediocre at best. Given their massive distributional problems, it is hardly surprising that the majority of the population in all three countries remains mired in poverty or economic vulnerability.

For countries in the Northern Triangle, the path towards a successful integration into the global economy is fraught with uncertainty. For all the opportunities that CAFTA-DR has opened up for these small economies, it is obvious than much more than free trade agreements will be needed if they are to thrive economically and significantly increase their development levels. Even CAFTA-DR has proved a mixed blessing –over the past few years, bilateral trade with the United States has grown a lot, but is consistently favorable to the United States. Unlike some of their neighbors to the South, such as Costa Rica and Panama, countries in the Northern Triangle remain stuck in a model of international insertion largely based on cheap labor, an option that has translated into a predominant role for the export of agricultural products and textiles and apparel. For instance, textiles and apparel comprise well over one half of US-bound exports in the case of El Salvador and Honduras. At the very least it is questionable that such a model will be sustainable in light of the economic emergence of China, India and even Vietnam.

If countries in the Northern Triangle are to prosper, they must tackle the truly difficult task of raising the productivity level of their labor force. This calls for a set of very difficult undertakings, including increasing education expenditures that are dismally low and inefficient. Today, almost three quarters of the workforce in the Northern Triangle still lack a complete secondary education, including almost one third that has not finished even the primary education. It also requires improving road and port infrastructure that is among the very worst in Latin America, and bringing research and development investments beyond the pitifully low levels that they have now. This is a point that deserves some emphasis. At 0.3% of GDP, the resources that Costa Rica invests in research and development are far and away the highest in Central America. Yet, that percentage is less than half the figure for Latin America and the Caribbean as a whole, and one-fifteenth the figure for Israel. The number of resident patent filings per million inhabitants in Guatemala is roughly on a par with that of Uganda or Zambia. You don't have to be a fortune-teller to foresee the difficulties that Guatemala will have to keep pace with the 21st Century.

Also, the region must lend a hand in myriad ways to small and medium enterprises that are 97% of firms in Central America and which only rarely sell their products abroad. Ultimately, the Northern Triangle must find a way to drastically reduce the more than 60% of the labor force (over 70% in Guatemala) that currently works in informal jobs with negligible productivity.

All this demands enormous public investments of different kinds and a state that works, which of course takes the discussion back to the question of fiscal robustness. Yet, unless countries in Northern Central America undertake these reforms, integration with the world economy will only consolidate the social and economic segmentation that afflicts them today, and the region's growing propensity to export its people.

For these countries, introducing the structural changes that are needed to enhance productivity, economic dynamism and opportunities is a tall order. It would be so even if they didn't have in remittances an economic shortcut that allows them if not to thrive, then at least to stay afloat. But they do. Today, remittances contribute 10% of GDP in Guatemala, nearly 17% in El Salvador, and over 18% in Honduras, a proportion that hasn't changed much over the past few years. The plain truth is that it is migrants that make the trek north that keep these economies viable. Bar a drastic tightening of migratory rules in the United States, this is unlikely to change for the foreseeable future. Sadly, given the difficulties involved in addressing structural economic weaknesses and the lack of obvious sources of sustainable growth, Northern Central America's economic future will most likely hinge on its ability to continue exporting its young people. In the absence of a dramatic change of heart by its political and economic elite, the region will have to give up its best hope for the future in order to have any kind of future.

Crime and violence: For all the gravity of the political and economic problems laid out in the previous paragraphs, there is little doubt that the most pressing challenge faced by the Northern Triangle and the one that truly sets the region apart concerns the extraordinarily high levels of crime. As has been said often over the past few years, the northern half of the Central American isthmus is now the most violent region in the world outside of active war zones. Homicide rates in the region are among the highest in the world, with recent figures in Honduras (87.3 murders per 100,000 people on average in 2010-13, although it came down slightly in 2013) and El Salvador (expected to approach nearly 100 per 100,000 this year) reaching unprecedented levels in Latin America and the Caribbean, if not the world. More than 120,000 Guatemalans, Hondurans and Salvadorans have died perished in the past ten years as a result of crime. Last year, Honduras alone had far more murders than the 28 member states of the European Union combined.

Murder rates are merely the most visible consequence of the problem. The proportion of households that have been victims of crime in the course of the past year is greater than one third in every country in the Northern Triangle. To this we have to add several other manifestations of violence whose magnitude we can only guess. Different estimates place well above 50,000 the number of members of youth gangs –known as *maras*— in all three countries. These gangs have a significant incidence in the region's violence levels, as well as a growing participation in supporting organized crime.

Indeed, violence levels in Northern Central America–notably in Guatemala and Honduras, less so in El Salvador-- cannot be understood but in terms of the pervasive presence of organized crime in the region, particularly drug trafficking. Close to 90% of the cocaine destined for the U.S. transits through the Central America and Mexico corridor. It is not coincidental that Central America exhibits the highest murder rates in the world.

The consequences of this tragedy are multifold, and go beyond the obvious human cost. There are economic implications, which become clear when we think that more than half the murder casualties in Central America are young men between 15 and 29 years old, at the peak of their productive and reproductive lives. The World Bank's recent estimation of the direct and indirect cost of violence in Central America put it at nearly 8% of the region's GDP.

Yet, it is the political consequences that I want to emphasize here. The perception that state authorities are unable to protect the citizen's most fundamental rights is visibly damaging the support for democratic institutions in Central America and becoming a breeding ground for authoritarian attitudes. According to a 2008 study by José Miguel Cruz, a scholar at Florida International University, 53% of the population in Guatemala, El Salvador and Honduras was willing to support a coup d'etat if it helped to solve insecurity problems, a reaction that no other social problem elicited. The Central American population –as frightened as it is eager for public order—is heeding carefully and often rewarding at the ballot box populist rhetoric that offers the "iron fist" and a cavalier attitude towards the rule of law to solve the problem.

This is unfortunate, for the record of "iron fist" solutions to crime is poor. Both Honduras and El Salvador offer a poignant reminder of this. In Honduras, the enactment since 2002 of successive legislative packages to deal with crime, with clear repressive overtones, has only made the situation worse. The 56 murders per 100,000 people that the country had in 2002 have climbed to nearly 90 today, the worst figure in the world. The Salvadoran experience is more complex, but equally unfortunate. In that country, the introduction of the "Iron Fist" and "Super Iron Fist" acts in 2003 and 2004 was unable to prevent the massive escalation of violence that preceded the adoption of a semi-official truce between the main youth gangs in 2012 and, later, a precipitous fall in the number of homicides. The collapse of the truce in 2014 has seen the return, with a vengeance, of three ills that seem to march apace – a virtual state of war between the gangs, widespread fear in society, and a heavy handed response from the government, which appears at a loss as to how to stop the vicious cycle of killings. August of 2015 ended with more than 900 homicides, making it the deadliest month since the end of the Civil War in El Salvador. In all likelihood, the return of the iron fist and, more worryingly, of the militarization of public security will not be more successful than previous iterations of the policy.

A second crucial political consequence is the weakening of the state and its legal powers. As is the case in certain regions of Mexico, in some places in Northern Central America that have been overrun by organized crime, it is debatable whether the state still enjoys the monopoly over legitimate coercion.

The consequences of the weakening of the state's writ are several. One of them is the growing tendency amongst the citizenry in these countries to defect from the public instruments to protect security, whose activation is considered useless or even counterproductive. This defection can take different shapes that range from the reluctance of the population to report crime, to the proliferation of private security firms, and the acceptance of lynching as a valid method to fight crime. Last but not least, many citizens of the Northern Triangle are defecting by leaving their country.

For all the tough talk about "iron fisted" solutions, a sustainable reduction of crime levels in the Northern Central America requires far more than the use of coercion. It demands a comprehensive policy combination that gives priority to reforming notoriously corrupt and inefficient police forces, introducing modern technology and information systems to sustain policy decisions, strengthening social ties and the organization of communities, and, above all, investing a lot more in education, health, housing and opportunities for the youth. Such is the road travelled by successful experiences in Latin American cities like Bogota and Sao Paulo, which have managed to slash violence levels in the past two decades. With 80 murders per 100,000 people, Bogota was one of the world's most dangerous cities in 1994; in 2014, with 17, it was one of the safest capitals in the Western Hemisphere. Balancing "zero tolerance" for crime with "zero tolerance" for social exclusion offers a way forward even in dire circumstances.

What is to be done? As is plain to see, the pathologies that hold back the Northern Triangle of Central America and drive many of its citizens to leave their countries are not just complex but deeply intertwined.

The penetration of organized crime, one of the most serious challenges of the region, provides a vivid example of the toxic interaction between these factors. The vulnerability of the countries in the Northern half of Central America to the ravages of organized crime is not simply the result of an accident of geography, of the peculiar misfortune of living equidistant from some of the largest drug producing countries as well as the single largest drug-consuming nation. Unfortunate as that may be, these countries are vulnerable to organized crime primarily because their fiscally anemic states are, in some cases, unable to exert effective control over their territory, thus creating an environment for crime syndicates to operate untrammeled. They are vulnerable, also, because their public institutions –starved of resources and debilitated by endemic corruption— are incapable of making the investments required to enhance the dynamism of the economy, prepare their countries for the 21st Century and, above all, enlarge the opportunities of young people to live a long, healthy and productive life. They are unable, that is, to prevent one of the calamities that lie at the core of the region's travails – that 25% of young people that are neither studying nor working, that have no stake in their societies, and that find it difficult to resist the pull of gangs and other criminal organizations. Moreover, these three Central American nations are vulnerable to organized crime because their law enforcement institutions have all but collapsed under the weight of venality and political interference and display a long history of turning a blind eye to the abuses of the powerful. These institutions are attractive to organized crime because they have long been instruments not of justice but of impunity. It is thus impossible to deal successfully with organized crime –or with the causes of large-scale migration, for that matter—unless all these issues are tackled in an integral, genuine, and sustained way.

Solving the predicament of the Northern Triangle requires that truly structural steps are taken, such as creating modern, progressive and robust tax systems; introducing real checks and balances; ending widespread impunity; and abandoning a patrimonial conception of the state, which blurs the lines between public and private interests. Needless to say, the impulse to do all this must come from within the countries, mainly from within political and economic elites that historically have fallen woefully short of their responsibilities. None of this can be corrected by international assistance alone. Yet, given the magnitude of the challenges, none of this can be corrected without international assistance.

The United States, in particular, can and should play an important role in supporting the necessary changes. For Washington paying more attention to the Northern Triangle of Central America is not a favor or an act of charity. In the case of a region that is showing disturbing signs of instability, that is a stone's throw away from the United States and that has already sent three million of its people to the shores of this country it could only be considered enlightened self-interest.

The following are some of the ways in which the United States could play a limited but meaningful role in helping the nations of the Northern Triangle help themselves:

Fund generously the Alliance for Prosperity in the Northern Triangle. The Alliance for Prosperity, whose funding is currently under the consideration of the US Congress, is a valuable and well-conceived program that is worthy of support. Above all, it is a sign that the United States cares about its neighbors and is actively trying to shape the future of a relationship –with Central America—that is doomed to be part of US policy debates, as has happened time and again over the past 150 years. The Alliance's strategic lines (stimulating the productive sector, developing opportunities for people, improving public safety and justice, and strengthening institutions) embody the long-term and integral approach that is essential in order to bring about structural change in Northern Central America and, hopefully, contain migratory flows to the United States. It would be a significant loss, not just to Central America, but also to US taxpayers, if as a result of bureaucratic or political tussles in Washington, the program sheds its holistic conception and winds up as yet another narrow counter narcotics effort. As mentioned above, development problems in the Northern Triangle are complex and mutually reinforcing. It is highly unlikely that any effort designed to tackle any one of them will have any impact if it fails to set in motion changes in other policy areas.

Helping rebuild law enforcement institutions in the Northern Triangle should be one the priorities of the Alliance. While, it ought to be acknowledged that rebuilding them is a generational endeavor, which only the countries themselves can undertake, assistance from the United States, as well as from Mexico, Colombia and other regional partners, can nonetheless play an important role. International assistance in this field can only hope to bring about visible changes if it focuses on a few urgent institutional programs that may exert a catalytic effect on the transformation of the image and efficacy of law enforcement bodies in the region. Particularly urgent tasks on which US assistance could have an impact include:

a) Improving internal control and anti-corruption units within law enforcement bodies;
b) Adopting modern information technologies (from regular victimization surveys to *CompStat*-like crime data gathering systems) as part of the policy making process;
c) Creating vetted units to handle complex multi-national investigations;

Improving investigation and prosecutorial capacities with regards to complex financial crimes. *Support Guatemala's CICIG and expand it*. The US government played no small part in the creation of CICIG in 2006. Even before its crucial role in the investigation that led to the resignation of President Pérez-Molina in Guatemala, the Commission had proved a valuable resource to carry out complex investigations that, almost certainly, were beyond the capabilities of Guatemala's law enforcement bodies. After eight years, the Commission can point to real successes in solving high-profile criminal cases, much as its efforts have on occasion been undermined by rulings by the local judiciary. Whatever criticism may be directed against CICIG, it remains a carefully vetted unit in a country in which the penetration of law enforcement institutions by crime syndicates is a serious problem. Despite the obvious displeasure of former President Pérez-Molina, CICIG's mandate was recently extended until September 2017. The international community's continued support –financial as much as political—for CICIG is vital not just for Guatemala, but also for the whole region. The experience of

CICIG provides an obvious blueprint for similar bodies that could and perhaps should be adopted in other countries of the Northern Triangle, notably Honduras.

Indeed, the option of expanding CICIG beyond the Guatemalan borders and turning it into a regional body, covering all three countries of Northern Central America, should be considered. Besides economies of scale, such a step could offer a solution to the thorny coordination issues that mar regional efforts against organized crime and diminish the effectiveness of the considerable flows of international assistance that support anti-crime efforts in Central America ($1.7 billion for the whole of Central America since 2003, according to research done by the Inter American Development Bank and the Washington Office for Latin America).

The model of CICIG offers a superior alternative to the plan, currently under consideration, to create an OAS-sponsored Mission of Support against Corruption and Impunity in Honduras (MACCIH by its acronym in Spanish). While not devoid of merits, the latter plan substitutes an elaborate set of functions to advise law enforcement institutions in Honduras for the robust investigation and prosecuting powers that have proved so crucial to CICIG's success in Guatemala. This is a glaring flaw. Nonetheless, if the political will to establish a CICIG-like body in Honduras proves impossible to secure, then the current proposal should be given the benefit of the doubt and its implementation ought to be carefully monitored by the international community.

Help small and medium enterprises (SMEs) take advantage of CAFTA-DR. SMEs are the great engines for the creation of employment in Central America. Yet, they seldom have access to international markets. Helping them make the most of the opportunities opened by free trade with the United States would be a major transformation on many levels. The funds to support such a program could be disbursed over several years and conditioned on Central American governments raising a matching sum from domestic sources. This exercise in co-responsibility should indeed become a general principle informing US-Central America relations.

Incentivize research and technology transfer in renewable energies. The development of renewable energies offers the promise of fruitful collaboration between the United States and Central America. At the very least, as advocated by the Partnership for the Americas Commission a few years ago, the US government—perhaps in partnership with other governments in the hemisphere—should establish a Renewable Energy Laboratory of the Americas in the isthmus, with the objective of promoting hemispheric cooperation on developing and transferring solar, wind, geothermal and cellulosic-biomass technologies. That would be an important step to help Central America develop one of the few sectors in which it has real long-term economic potential.

Insist on structural reforms. There are clear limits to what even a generous and soundly conceived program of foreign assistance can achieve in Northern Central America. The lion's share of the task of transforming Guatemala, Honduras and El Salvador must be borne by the citizens and, above all, the elites of these countries. It is a legitimate question whether the US Government will find in the current political elites in the Northern Triangle the suitable partners to make the effort of assisting the region worthwhile. There are no easy answers to that question. The case of President Pérez-Molina in Guatemala and the unprecedented popular mobilization against corruption in Honduras suggest that some of the best partners are to be found in the region's increasingly assertive civil societies. One can also point to brave, isolated reformers that are willing to defy impossible odds to bring about institutional change. The examples of Guatemala's former Attorney General Claudia Paz y Paz, police reformer Hellen Mack, and the prosecutors and judges that recently stood up to Otto Pérez-Molina in Guatemala come to mind. Also worth mentioning is the experience of the members of the Constitutional Court in El Salvador, which over the past few years have shown their willingness to assert their political independence and reform the Salvadoran political system. Identifying those champions of reform is difficult but possible. In any case, it is essential if external efforts to help these countries are to have any chance to succeed.

I will submit that when it comes to political partners in the region, the US Government can gauge their seriousness according to two basic criteria: first, their readiness to push for robust and progressive tax systems; and, second, their sincerity about introducing checks and balances and promoting judicial independence, without which any effort against corruption and impunity is doomed to failure. Hence, attempts to pack the Supreme Court or to introduce indefinite reelection, for instance, ought to be taken for what they are – preludes to the corruption, power abuse and impunity that have sadly been the historical norm in much of Central America. This behavior is simply inimical to any real effort to establish the rule of law in the countries of the isthmus.

Introducing progressive tax reform and real checks and balances on executive power are the crux of the matter in the Northern Triangle. If the United States is serious about helping Guatemala, Honduras and El Salvador, it should not be shy about demanding those structural changes.

Central America needs the generous help of the United States, but it must do its share of the task if it is to have a future, one in which its young people hopefully will choose to build their lives in their own country.

In: Migration of Unaccompanied Children … ISBN: 978-1-63484-604-2
Editor: Angie Hopkins

Chapter 4

STATEMENT OF DUNCAN WOOD, DIRECTOR, MEXICO INSTITUTE, WOODROW WILSON INTERNATIONAL CENTER FOR SCHOLARS. HEARING ON "ONGOING MIGRATION FROM CENTRAL AMERICA: AN EXAMINATION OF FISCAL YEAR 2015 APPREHENSIONS"*

INTRODUCTION

The dramatic spike in the number of unaccompanied minors arriving at the U.S.- Mexico border in the summer of 2014 raised public awareness in the United States of a tendency that had in fact been underway for a number of years. Since the late 2000s, as Mexican undocumented migration to the United States entered into steady decline, a growing number of Central American migrants have been making their way through Mexico towards the United States. This transmigration phenomenon reflects increasingly harsh and violent conditions in many of the countries of Central America, as well as growing desperation brought about by poverty and the failure of national economies, as noted in previous Senate HSGAC hearings.

---

* This is an edited, reformatted and augmented version of a statement presented October 21, 2015 before the Senate Committee on Homeland Security and Governmental Affairs.

Partly in response to this phenomenon, and partly in response to the intense criticism that was aimed at the Mexican government in the wake of ongoing abuses of Central American migrant rights, in July 2014, Mexican President Enrique Peña Nieto launched the *Programa Frontera Sur* (PFS or South Border Program) with two main official objectives: first, to protect migrants who enter Mexico, and second, to manage the ports of entry in a way that promotes the security and prosperity of the region. The PFS involves a massive investment in infrastructure and procedures that represents a credible attempt to impose some sense of order in Mexico's southern region, and gives the Mexican state a highly visible presence in an area that has traditionally been ignored or neglected by Mexico City.

It is important to recognize here the complexity of the task at hand. Mexico's southern border region is a varied and complicated area, with mountains and jungle, extreme poverty but great natural riches, and an extraordinary diversity of indigenous cultures. The border itself is defined by both river and land crossings, with three major rivers on the southern border: the Rio Suchiate and Rio Negro/Usumacinta along the border with Guatemala, and the Arroyo Azul/Rio Hondo with Belize. The topography of the region alone makes complete control of cross-border traffic an impossible task. To complicate matters further, there are a number of small urban centers at the border, with uncontrolled border crossings existing right beside the formal border management facilities.

Indeed the number of formal crossing points that exist along the border is dwarfed by informal crossings. Many of these are crucial for local commerce and support the local economy. One of the most important observations from recent Wilson Center tours of Mexico´s southern border is that official strategies to contain illegal flows need to take into consideration the needs of the local community, so as to not interrupt these economies and trade. In addition to protecting the livelihoods of local families, this is important for two further reasons. First, local communities have a history of protesting projects that damage their interests, and this can force governments to back down. There are stories of this on both sides of the border, in a number of cases. Second, securing the cooperation of the local community is crucial to the effective gathering of intelligence about illicit flows and routes in the vicinity. In these cases, a military or police presence to deter the trafficking of weapons, arms and people is preferable, as most of the traffic is back and forth, a perfectly natural phenomenon for neighboring communities.

The case of Ciudad Hidalgo-Tecun Uman is illustrative. The presence of both an official border crossing on the Mexican side and multiple informal crossings allows those who wish to cross formally into Mexico to do so, while those who prefer to circumvent Mexican authorities face few barriers. After the devastation of Hurricane Stan in 2005, Mexico's national water commission, CONAGUA, built strong and high levees on the Mexican side of the Rio Suchiate in the Ciudad Hidalgo area. Although appreciative of the protection against the devastation of future natural disasters, the local community protested that their access to the river and its informal crossings had been impeded. In response, the CONAGUA built a pedestrian and small, light vehicle pathway over the levee, so that the informal commerce could continue. This was a story that was repeated several times during the Wilson Center tours of the border regions: if local community concerns are not heeded, then authorities have come to expect that protests and blockades of official crossings and border installations will result.

Furthermore, it is crucial to recognize that Mexico's attempts to begin to assert some control over its southern border are still at a preliminary stage. Although impressive progress has been made over the past few years, the *Program Frontera Sur* is very much a work in progress, and we should not expect it to provide a comprehensive solution to undocumented migration nor flows of illicit goods. However, the work undertaken thus far has delivered significant results, and it is at last possible to talk about meaningful action taking place on North America's southern border.

MEXICO EYES ITS SOUTHERN BORDER

Until very recently, Mexico's border with Guatemala and Belize was poorly marked, with inadequate attention paid to demarcating the exact border. However, in recent years, the Mexico-Guatemala *Comision Internacional de Limites Y Aguas* (CILA or International Boundary and Waters Commission) has made an impressive effort dedicating resources to tracing and marking the border, building and maintaining border monuments that definitively show the limit of Mexican territory. It is vital to emphasize the central role played by the CILA: not only is it the government agency that handles most of the day-to-day border management in the south, it is a vitally important repository of on-the-ground knowledge and understanding.

In 2013, the CILA carried out an impressive survey of Mexico's southern border that represents the best effort to date at recording both formal and informal border crossings. The survey identified eight formal border crossings with Guatemala, as well as fifty-seven informal crossing points; with Belize, it noted two formal crossings, and one informal (near the Mexican town of La Union). This latter figure is likely inaccurate; the border between the two countries is 288 kilometers in length, and the only formal crossings are near the Mexican city of Chetumal and the Belize city of Corozal at the extreme east of the border. Although the rest of the border region is sparsely populated, it is likely that there are other informal crossing points that have not been identified to date.

The 2013 CILA survey also gave an estimate of the daily traffic crossing the border at the formal crossing points. Although these figures are based on the best guesses of border personnel, rather than a scientific study, they offer a useful estimate of infrastructure and staffing needs at the official border points. Furthermore, the survey recorded each of the Mexican government agencies that are represented at each official crossing, along with their current staffing levels. Most importantly, the survey identified the most important challenges and problems at each of the formal crossings, on both sides of the border. It is hoped that this survey is taken into consideration when future investment decisions are made.

The *Programa Frontera Sur* focuses on five different goals to be able to assert greater control over the southern border region. These goals are:

- Regular and Ordered Migration
- Improvements in Infrastructure, for border security and migration
- Protecting Migrants
- Regional Shared Responsibility
- Interagency Coordination

The recent Wilson Center tours of the southern border have verified that there has been significant progress in each of these areas, and the result has been a much higher visibility of Mexican government agencies throughout the south.

New Efforts to Control Migration

As part of the PFS, the Mexican migration authorities have been implementing a number of new initiatives to try to impose some order on the transmigration phenomenon. First, two new visas have been issued for Guatemalan and Belizean citizens who wish to visit Mexico. The *Tarjeta de*

Visitante Regional (TVR or Regional Visitor Card) allows visitors to cross into border municipalities with an unlimited number of entries, each of which is limited to a 72 hour period and is valid for up to 5 years. Since 2014, this visa has been free of charge (prior to this it cost 295 pesos). For those people who wish to work in the border region, the government issues a *Tarjeta de Visitante Trabajador Fronterizo* (TVTF or Border Worker Visitor Card) which costs 305 pesos. In 2015 thus far, almost 80,000 people were granted the TVR visa, and around 11,000 TVTF visas. The PFS mandated simpler application procedures and new offices for issuing the permits. These permits allow those who wish to cross formally into Mexico to do so in an entirely legal way. More importantly, the regional visa system is an attempt to formalize what had hitherto been a largely unsupervised phenomenon. They do not, however, address the issue of those who are crossing Mexico to get to the United States.

The Mexican government's attempts to address transmigration have focused on building new infrastructure, both at the border itself and at inland locations. Under the PFS, the ten border crossings are being enhanced, and five *Centros de Atención Integral al Tránsito Fronterizo* (Comprehensive Border Crossing Attention Centers), are being built at remote locations, on major routes northward. These new, multimodal, interagency facilities are impressive, with multiple government agencies working side by side. At each facility Mexican customs, immigration, health, agriculture, police and military agencies are represented.

In addition to border-control infrastructure, Mexico has also undertaken the construction of new migrant holding centers (*estaciones migratorias*) where migrants who have been detained in Mexican territory can be processed for "assisted return" or deportation. The difference between these two categories in Mexico is a legal matter. Migrants are only deported if they have broken Mexican laws, whereas migrants who lack the proper papers are repatriated with the help of Mexican government agencies. The speed of this varies enormously, and much depends on the cooperation of the consuls from Central American states to expedite the process.

Despite many complaints and some damning reports from civil society groups about the conditions and treatment of migrants in these centers, a Wilson Center research group was favorably impressed by a tour of the *Estacion Migratoria Siglo XXI* in March of 2015. However, on a later visit to a smaller processing center at La Trinitaria, Chiapas, there appeared to be a brazen disregard for migrant rights where registration forms were pre-filled before being given to the migrants, including the section of the form that asks whether the individual is requesting refugee status.

Table 1. Regional Visitor Permits (TVR) issued in 2015 by state and place of issue

País de residencia/ Entidad federativa/ Punto de expedición	Enero	Febrero	Marzo	Abril	Mayo	Junio	Julio	Agosto	Total
Total general	**9 110**	**9 420**	**12 832**	**9 133**	**9 334**	**11 220**	**10 149**	**8 552**	**79 750**
Total Guatemala	**8 808**	**9 238**	**12 599**	**8 943**	**9 084**	**10 994**	**9 930**	**8 345**	**77 941**
Chiapas	**8 177**	**8 717**	**11 915**	**8 445**	**8 580**	**10 313**	**9 408**	**7 807**	**73 362**
Carmen Xhan	435	637	696	597	589	635	446	773	**4 808**
Ciudad Cuauhtémoc	1 499	1 283	1 663	1 558	1 601	1 550	1 828	1 550	**12 532**
Ciudad Hidalgo	2 597	2 818	3 961	2 686	2 701	3 483	2 713	2 421	**23 380**
Talismán	3 159	3 541	5 136	3 241	3 430	4 207	4 161	2 997	**29 872**
Unión Juárez [2]	487	438	459	363	259	438	260	66	**2 770**
Tabasco	**631**	**521**	**684**	**498**	**504**	**681**	**522**	**538**	**4 579**
El Ceibo	631	521	684	498	504	681	522	538	**4 579**
Total Belice	**302**	**182**	**233**	**190**	**250**	**226**	**219**	**207**	**1 809**
Quintana Roo	**302**	**182**	**233**	**190**	**250**	**226**	**219**	**207**	**1 809**
Chetumal, Subteniente López	302	182	233	190	250	226	219	207	**1 809**

Table 2. Visiting Border Worker Program (TVTF) permits issued 2015 by state and place of issue

País de residencia/ Entidad federativa / Punto de expedición	Enero	Febrero	Marzo	Abril	Mayo	Junio	Julio	Agosto	Total
Total general [2]	**2 352**	**1 339**	**1 358**	**1 332**	**1 323**	**1 392**	**973**	**773**	**10 842**
Total Guatemala	**2 349**	**1 339**	**1 357**	**1 332**	**1 323**	**1 392**	**973**	**771**	**10 836**
Chiapas	**2 345**	**1 336**	**1 355**	**1 331**	**1 308**	**1 392**	**969**	**769**	**10 805**
Carmen Xhan	-	-	-	-	-	-	-	-	**-**
Ciudad Cuauhtémoc	462	117	86	198	184	166	204	118	**1 535**
Ciudad Hidalgo	1 034	947	1 092	734	762	807	535	411	**6 322**
Talismán	849	272	177	399	362	419	230	240	**2 948**
Unión Juárez	-	-	-	-	-	-	-	-	**-**
Tabasco	**4**	**3**	**2**	**1**	**15**	**-**	**4**	**2**	**31**
El Ceibo	4	3	2	1	15	-	4	2	**31**
Total Belice	**3**	**-**	**1**	**-**	**-**	**-**	**-**	**2**	**6**
Quintana Roo	**3**	**-**	**1**	**-**	**-**	**-**	**-**	**2**	**6**
Chetumal, Subteniente López	3	-	1	-	-	-	-	2	**6**

Table 3. Central American returns (Belize, Costa Rica, El Salvador, Guatemala, Honduras, Nicaragua, Panamá) 2015 Jan-Aug

Deportations	Assisted Returns
780	88636

Source: Government of Mexico, Boletin Mensual de Estadisticas Migratorias 2015, INM.

Table 4. Number and percentages of deportations and assisted returns by country of origin 2015 Jan-Aug

Country	Number of deportations	Percentage	Assisted Returns	Percentage
Belice	12	1.54%	19	0.02%
Costa Rica	3	0.38%	1	0.00%
El Salvador	119	15.26%	16996	19.18%
Guatemala	473	60.64%	39851	44.96%
Honduras	171	21.92%	30883	34.84%
Nicaragua	2	0.26%	884	1%
Panama	0	0.00%	2	0.00%
Total	780	100.00%	88636	100.00%

Source: Government of Mexico, Boletin Mensual de Estadisticas Migratorias 2015, INM.

Despite many complaints and some damning reports from civil society groups about the conditions and treatment of migrants in these centers, a Wilson Center research group was favorably impressed by a tour of the *Estacion Migratoria Siglo XXI* in March of 2015. However, on a later visit to a smaller processing center at La Trinitaria, Chiapas, there appeared to be a brazen disregard for migrant rights where registration forms were pre-filled before being given to the migrants, including the section of the form that asks whether the individual is requesting refugee status.

Naturally, migrants have learned quickly about the location of these centers, and alternate routes have been identified to circumvent them. Often, these other routes are well known to the authorities, and Mexico is investing in mobile checkpoints that can cover some, but not all, of the alternative paths. As is the case with migration around the world, shutting off one route simply pushes migrants to take different, often more difficult and dangerous paths though southern Mexico.

During our research, we asked both authorities and civil society groups about the unaccompanied minors phenomenon. We were told that the dramatic rise in numbers last year was not being repeated in 2015, but that there are still significant numbers moving northwards.

Table 5. Number of Unaccompanied Central American Minors, 2015 Jan-Aug

Country	January	February	March	April	May	June	July	August	Total
Belize	0	0	0	0	0	1	0	0	1
El Salvador	94	155	189	195	263	243	299	308	1746
Guatemala	471	600	629	631	726	751	803	748	5359
Honduras	181	251	321	285	337	351	377	315	2418
Nicaragua	0	3	0	1	2	1	2	1	10
Panama	0	1	1	0	0	0	0	0	2
Total	746	1010	1140	1112	1328	1347	1481	1372	9536

Source: Government of Mexico, Boletin Mensual de Estadisticas Migratorias 2015, INM.

The advances that have been made in Mexican border infrastructure are especially impressive when compared with the relative lack of order on the Guatemalan side. At all of the formal crossings between Mexico and Guatemala, the Mexican government is investing heavily in developing border control capacity, while its Guatemalan counterpart appears to be doing nothing to improve its own measures.

The investment in infrastructure and procedures on the part of the Mexican government is indeed impressive, and can be understood both as an attempt to gain control of illicit and licit flows of goods and people north from Central America, as well as a clear effort to deter illicit flows by raising the costs of transportation of drugs and weapons. There is also clearly an effort to diminish the flows of undocumented migrants, and the existence of more, and better-equipped migration stations and offices is surely pushing migrants crossing from Central America to find other routes.

In the case of Guatemala, the Mexican government appears to have placed a heavy bet on its counterpart following through on commitments to complete border infrastructure projects, with little evidence that those commitments will be honored in the near future. However, in the case of Belize, the Mexican government has found a partner that has thus far cooperated ably, and there appears to be a common desire to regularize flows.

Despite this spirit of cooperation and the infrastructure and procedural achievements by the Mexican government, our journey along the border revealed that there are still major challenges to be overcome. First, the sheer number of informal crossings from both Guatemala and Belize almost beggars belief, with trails, roads, and river crossings either policed infrequently by just the military (to impede the flow of weapons and drugs) or not at all. Some informal crossings are signposted by locals who hope to derive an income by permitting access to paths through the jungle; others are hidden away from view. These informal crossings often thwart the efforts of the Mexican government to control flows as they lead to other routes that circumvent border controls, both at the border itself and inland. In fact, we saw a number of examples where roads provided short cuts that bypassed the largest control centers on major highways. The solution clearly lies in a combination of fixed-location controls and more mobile units that can be used to deter the use of alternative routes.

Overall, the recent Wilson Center tours of Mexico's southern border observed a considerable and increasing formalization of traffic and a much more visible presence of government agencies. This involves multi-million dollar investments in infrastructure, as well as considerable planning. An important recognition is that this is an evolving situation. As Mexico invests more in border infrastructure, and also learns and adapts according to its experience and interaction with foreign governments, migrants, businesses, communities and organized crime, we will see many changes, But there is certainly a strategy in place, one that seeks to assert the authority, and more importantly, the presence, of the State along Mexico´s southern border lands. It is encouraging to see how far Mexico has come, but it is also daunting when one considers how many challenges remain, many of which are outside of Mexico's control, especially when one considers the weakness and many problems facing its southern neighbors.

INDEX

A

B

C

D

E

F

G

H

I

O

P

Q

R

S

T

U

V

W

Y